POETRY FIRST EDITIONS

Poems,
Chiefly in the
Scottish Dialect

ROBERT BURNS

8

ROBERT BURNS (1759–96)

Poems, Chiefly in the Scottish Dialect
first published 1786

ROBERT BURNS

Poems, Chiefly in the Scottish Dialect

with a Note on the Text by
Michael Schmidt

PENGUIN BOOKS

PENGUIN BOOKS

Published by the Penguin Group
Penguin Books Ltd, 27 Wrights Lane, London w8 5tz, England
Penguin Putnam Inc., 375 Hudson Street, New York, New York 10014, USA
Penguin Books Australia Ltd, Ringwood, Victoria, Australia
Penguin Books Canada Ltd, 10 Alcorn Avenue, Toronto, Ontario, Canada m4v 3b2
Penguin Books (NZ) Ltd, Private Bag 102902, NSMC, Auckland, New Zealand

Penguin Books Ltd, Registered Offices: Harmondsworth, Middlesex, England

Published in Penguin Books 1999
1 3 5 7 9 10 8 6 4 2

The cover shows a detail from *Flowers in a Roemer with a Mouse Eating an Ear of Corn*,
seventeenth century, by Clara Peeters (photo: Christies Images)

The moral right of the author of the Note on the Text has been asserted

Set in 11/14 pt PostScript Monotype Baskerville
Typeset by Rowland Phototypesetting Ltd, Bury St Edmunds, Suffolk
Printed in England by Clays Ltd, St Ives plc

The Simple Bard, unbroke by rules of Art,
He pours the wild effusions of the heart:
And if inspir'd, 'tis Nature's pow'rs inspire;
Her's all the melting thrill, and her's the kindling fire.

ANONYMOUS

PREFACE

The following trifles are not the production of the Poet, who, with all the advantages of learned art, and perhaps amid the elegancies and idlenesses of upper life, looks down for a rural theme, with an eye to Theocritus or Virgil. To the Author of this, these and other celebrated names their countrymen are, in their original languages, 'A fountain shut up, and a book sealed'. Unacquainted with the necessary requisites for commencing Poet by rule, he sings the sentiments and manners, he felt and saw in himself and his rustic compeers around him, in his and their native language. Though a Rhymer from his earliest years, at least from the earliest impulses of the softer passions, it was not till very lately, that the applause, perhaps the partiality, of Friendship, wakened his vanity so far as to make him think any thing of his was worth showing; and none of the following works were ever composed with a view to the press. To amuse himself with the little creations of his own fancy, amid the toil and fatigues of a laborious life; to transcribe the various feelings, the loves, the griefs, the hopes, the fears, in his own breast; to find some kind of counterpoise to the struggles of a world, always an alien scene, a task uncouth to the poetical mind; these were his motives for courting the Muses, and in these he found Poetry to be its own reward.

Now that he appears in the public character of an Author, he does it with fear and trembling. So dear is fame to the rhyming tribe, that even he, an obscure, nameless Bard, shrinks aghast, at the thought of being branded as 'An impertinent blockhead, obtruding his nonsense on the world; and because he can make a shift to jingle a few doggerel, Scotch rhymes together, looks upon himself as a Poet of no small consequence forsooth.'

It is an observation of that celebrated Poet,* whose divine Elegies do honor to our language, our nation, and our species, that 'Humility has depressed many a genius to a hermit, but never raised one to fame.' If any Critic catches at the word *genius*, the Author tells him, once for all, that he certainly looks upon himself as possest of some poetic abilities, otherwise his publishing in the manner he has done, would be a manœuvre below the worst character, which, he hopes, his worst enemy will ever give him: but to the genius of a Ramsay, or the glorious dawnings of the poor, unfortunate Ferguson, he, with equal unaffected sincerity, declares, that, even in his highest pulse of vanity, he has not the most distant pretensions. These two justly admired Scotch Poets he has often had in his eye in the following pieces; but rather with a view to kindle at their flame, than for servile imitation.

To his Subscribers, the Author returns his most sincere thanks. Not the mercenary bow over a counter, but the heart-throbbing gratitude of the Bard, conscious how much he is indebted to Benevolence and Friendship, for gratifying him, if he deserves it, in that dearest wish of every poetic bosom – to be distinguished. He begs his readers, particularly the Learned and the Polite, who may honor him with a perusal, that they will make every allowance for Education and Circumstances of Life: but, if after a fair, candid, and impartial criticism, he shall stand convicted of Dulness and Nonsense, let him be done by, as he would in that case do by others – let him be condemned, without mercy, to contempt and oblivion.

* Shenstone.

CONTENTS

The Twa Dogs
A TALE

'Twas in that place o' Scotland's isle;
That bears the name o' auld king Coil,
Upon a bonie day in June,
When wearing thro' the afternoon,
Twa Dogs, that were na thrang at hame,
Forgather'd ance upon a time.

The first I'll name, they ca'd him *Cæsar*,
Was keepet for His Honor's pleasure;
His hair, his size, his mouth, his lugs,
Shew'd he was nane o' Scotland's dogs,
But whalpet some place far abroad,
Where sailors gang to fish for Cod.

His locked, letter'd, braw brass-collar
Shew'd him the *gentleman* an' *scholar*;
But tho' he was o' high degree,
The fient a pride na pride had he,
But wad hae spent an hour caressan,
Ev'n wi' a Tinkler-gipsey's *messan*:
At Kirk or Market, Mill or Smiddie,
Nae tawted *tyke*, tho' e'er sae duddie,
But he wad stan't, as glad to see him,
An' stroan't on stanes an' hillocks wi' him.

The tither was a *ploughman's collie*,
A rhyming, ranting, raving billie,
Wha for his friend an' comrade had him,
And in his freaks had *Luath* ca'd him,
After some dog in *Higbland sang*,*
Was made lang syne, lord knows how lang.

He was a gash an' faithfu' *tyke*,
As ever lap a sheugh or dyke.
His honest, sonsie, baws'nt face,
Ay gat him friends in ilka place;
His breast was white, his towzie back,
Weel clad wi' coat o' glossy black;
His gawsie tail, wi' upward curl,
Hung owre his hurdies wi' a swirl.

Nae doubt but they were fain o' ither,
An' unco pack an' thick thegither;
Wi' social nose whyles snuff'd an' snowket;
Whyles mice and modewurks they howket;
Whyles scour'd awa in lang excursion,
An' worry'd ither in diversion;
Till tir'd at last wi' mony a farce,
They set them down upon their arse,
An' there began a lang digression
About the *lords o' the creation*.

CÆSAR

I've aften wonder'd, honest *Luath*,
What sort o' life poor dogs like you have;
An' when the *gentry's* life I saw,
What way *poor bodies* liv'd ava.

---

* Cuchullin's dog in Ossian's *Fingal*.

Our *Laird* gets in his racked rents,
His coals, his kane, an' a' his stents:
He rises when he likes himsel;
His flunkies answer at the bell;
He ca's his coach; he ca's his horse;
He draws a bonie, silken purse
As lang's my tail, whare thro' the steeks,
The yellow letter'd *Geordie* keeks.

Frae morn to een it's nought but toiling,
At baking, roasting, frying, boiling;
An' tho' the gentry first are steghan,
Yet ev'n the *ha' folk* fill their peghan
Wi' sauce, ragouts, an' sic like trashtrie,
That's little short o' downright wastrie.
Our *Whipper-in*, wee, blastet wonner,
Poor worthless elf, it eats a dinner,
Better than ony *Tenant-man*
His Honor has in a' the lan':
An' what poor *Cot-folk* pit their painch in,
I own it's past my comprehension.

LUATH

Trowth, Cæsar, whyles their fash't enough;
A *Cotter* howkan in a sheugh,
Wi' dirty stanes biggan a dyke,
Bairan a quarry, an' sic like,
Himsel, a wife, he thus sustains,
A smytrie o' wee, duddie weans,
An' nought but his han'-daurk, to keep
Them right an' tight in thack an' raep.

An' when they meet wi' fair disasters,
Like loss o' health or want o' masters,
Ye maist wad think, a wee touch langer,
An' they maun starve o' cauld and hunger:
But how it comes, I never kent yet,
They're maistly wonderfu' contented;
An' buirdly chiels, and clever hizzies,
Are bred in sic a way as this is.

CÆSAR

But then, to see how ye're negleket,
How huff'd, an' cuff'd, an' disrespeket!
L—d man, our gentry care as little
For *delvers, ditchers,* an' sic cattle;
They gang as saucy by poor folk,
As I wad by a stinkan brock.

I've notic'd, on our Laird's *court-day,*
An' mony a time my heart's been wae,
Poor *tenant bodies,* scant o' cash,
How they maun thole a *factor's* snash;
He'll stamp an' threaten, curse an' swear,
He'll *apprehend* them, *poind* their gear;
While they maun stan', wi' aspect humble,
An' hear it a', an' fear an' tremble!

I see how folk live that hae riches;
But surely poor-folk maun be wretches!

LUATH

They're no sae wretched 's ane wad think;
Tho' constantly on poortith's brink,
They're sae accustom'd wi' the sight,
The view o't gies them little fright.

Then chance and fortune are sae guided,
They're ay in less or mair provided;
An' tho' fatigu'd wi' close employment,
A blink o' rest 's a sweet enjoyment.

The dearest comfort o' their lives,
Their grushie weans an' faithfu' wives;
The *prattling things* are just their pride,
That sweetens a' their fire side.

An' whyles twalpennie-worth o' *nappy*
Can mak the bodies unco happy;
They lay aside their private cares,
To mind the Kirk and State affairs;
They'll talk o' *patronage* an' *priests*,
Wi' kindling fury i' their breasts,
Or tell what new taxation's comin,
An' ferlie at the folk in Lon'on.

As bleak-fac'd Hallowmass returns,
They get the jovial, rantan *Kirns*,
When *rural life*, of ev'ry station,
Unite in common recreation;
Love blinks, Wit slaps, an' social Mirth
Forgets there's *care* upo' the earth.

That *merry day* the year begins,
They bar the door on frosty win's;
The nappy reeks wi' mantling ream,
An' sheds a heart-inspiring steam;
The luntan pipe, an' sneeshin mill,
Are handed round wi' right guid will;

The cantie, auld folks, crackan crouse,
The young anes rantan thro' the house –
My heart has been sae fain to see them,
That I for joy hae barket wi' them.

   Still it's owre true that ye hae said,
Sic game is now owre aften play'd;
There's monie a creditable *stock*
O' decent, honest, fawsont folk,
Are riven out baith root an' branch,
Some rascal's pridefu' greed to quench,
Wha thinks to knit himsel the faster
In favor wi' some *gentle Master*,
Wha aiblins thrang a *parliamentin*,
For Britain's guid his saul indentin –

CÆSAR

Haith lad ye little ken about it;
For Britain's guid! guid faith! I doubt it.
Say rather, gaun as Premiers lead him,
An' saying *aye* or *no*'s they bid him:
At Operas an' Plays parading,
Mortgaging, gambling, masquerading:
Or maybe, in a frolic daft,
To Hague or Calais takes a waft,
To make a *tour* an' tak a whirl,
To learn *bon ton* an' see the worl'.

   There, at Vienna or Versailles,
He rives his father's auld entails;
Or by Madrid he takes the rout,
To thrum *guittars* an' fecht wi' nowt;
Or down *Italian Vista* startles,
Wh——re-hunting amang groves o' myrtles:

Then bowses drumlie *German-water*,
To mak himsel look fair and fatter,
An' purge the bitter ga's an' cankers,
O' curst *Venetian* b—res an' ch—ncres.

For Britain's guid! for her destruction!
Wi' dissipation, feud an' faction!

LUATH

Hech man! dear sirs! is that the gate,
They waste sae mony a braw estate!
Are we sae foughten and harass'd
For gear to gang that gate at last!

O would they stay aback frae courts,
An' please themsels wi' countra sports,
It wad for ev'ry ane be better,
The *Laird*, the *Tenant*, an' the *Cotter!*
For thae frank, rantan, ramblan billies,
Fient haet o' them 's ill hearted fellows;
Except for breakin o' their timmer,
Or speakin lightly o' their *Limmer*,
Or shootin of a hare or moorcock,
The ne'er-a-bit they're ill to poor folk.

But will ye tell me, master *Cæsar*,
Sure *great folk's* life's a life o' pleasure?
Nae cauld nor hunger e'er can steer them,
The vera thought o't need na fear them.

CÆSAR

L—d man, were ye but whyles where I am,
The *gentles* ye wad neer envy them!

It's true, they need na starve or sweat,
Thro' Winter's cauld, or Summer's heat;
They've nae sair-wark to craze their banes,
An' fill *auld-age* wi' grips an' granes;
But *human-bodies* are sic fools,
For a' their colledges an' schools,
That when nae *real* ills perplex them,
They *mak* enow themsels to vex them;
An' ay the less they hae to sturt them,
In like proportion, less will hurt them.

A country fellow at the pleugh,
His *acre's* till'd, he's right eneugh;
A country girl at her wheel,
Her *dizzen's* done, she's unco weel;
But Gentlemen, an' Ladies warst,
Wi' ev'n down *want o' wark* are curst.
They loiter, lounging, lank an' lazy;
Tho' deil-haet ails them, yet uneasy;
Their days, insipid, dull an' tasteless,
Their nights, unquiet, lang an' restless.

An' ev'n their sports, their balls an' races,
Their galloping thro' public places,
There's sic parade, sic pomp an' art,
The joy can scarcely reach the heart.

The *Men* cast out in *party-matches*,
Then sowther a' in deep debauches.
Ae night, they're mad wi' drink an' wh—ring,
Niest day their life is past enduring.

The *Ladies* arm-in-arm in clusters,
As great an' gracious a' as sisters;
But hear their *absent thoughts* o' ither,
They're a run deils an' jads thegither.
Whyles, owre the wee bit cup an' platie,
They sip the *scandal-potion* pretty;
Or lee-lang nights, wi' crabbet leuks,
Pore owre the devil's *pictur'd beuks*;
Stake on a chance a farmer's stackyard,
An' cheat like ony *unhang'd blackguard*.

There's some exceptions, man an' woman;
But this is Gentry's life in common.

By this, the sun was out o' sight,
An' darker gloamin brought the night:
The *bum-clock* humm'd wi' lazy drone,
The kye stood rowtan i' the loan;
When up they gat an' shook their lugs,
Rejoic'd they were na *men* but *dogs*;
An' each took off his several way,
Resolv'd to meet some ither day.

Scotch Drink

Gie him strong Drink *until he wink,*
That's sinking in despair;
An' liquor *guid to fire his bluid,*
That's prest wi' grief an' care:
There let him bowse an' deep carouse,
Wi' bumpers flowing o'er,
Till he forgets his loves *or* debts,
An' minds his griefs no more.

SOLOMON'S PROVERBS, xxxi, 6, 7

Let other Poets raise a fracas
'Bout vines, an' wines, an' druken *Bacchus*,
An' crabbed names an' stories wrack us,
      An' grate our lug,
I sing the juice *Scotch bear* can mak us,
      In glass or jug.
O thou, my Muse! guid, auld Scotch Drink!
Whether thro' wimplin worms thou jink,
Or, richly brown, ream owre the brink,
      In glorious faem,
Inspire me, till I *lisp* an' *wink*,
      To sing thy name!

Let husky Wheat the haughs adorn,
And Aits set up their awnie horn,
An' Pease an' Beans, at een or morn,
      Perfume the plain,
Leeze me on thee *John Barleycorn*,
      Thou king o' grain!

On thee aft Scotland chows her cood,
In souple scones, the wale o' food!
Or tumbling in the boiling flood
      Wi' kail an' beef;
But when thou pours thy strong *heart's blood*,
      There thou shines chief.

   Food fills the wame, an' keeps us livin;
Tho' life's a gift no worth receivin,
When heavy-dragg'd wi' pine an' grievin;
      But oil'd by thee,
The wheels o' life gae down-hill, scrievin,
      Wi' rattlin glee.

   Thou clears the head o' doited Lear;
Thou chears the heart o' drooping Care;
Thou strings the nerves o' Labor-fair,
      At's weary toil;
Thou ev'n brightens dark Despair,
      Wi' gloomy smile.

   Aft, clad in massy, siller weed,
Wi' Gentles thou erects thy head;
Yet humbly kind, in time o' need,
      The *poor man's* wine;
His wee drap pirratch, or his bread,
      Thou kitchens fine.

   Thou art the life o' public haunts;
But thee, what were our fairs and rants?
Ev'n godly meetings o' the saunts,
      By thee inspir'd,
When gaping they besiege the *tents*,
      Are doubly fir'd.

That *merry night* we get the corn in,
O sweetly, then, thou reams the horn in!
Or reekan on a *New-year-mornin*
     In cog or bicker,
An' just a wee drap *sp'ritual burn* in,
     An' gusty sucker!

When Vulcan gies his bellys breath,
An' Ploughmen gather wi' their graith,
O rare! to see thee fizz an' freath
     I' the lugget caup!
Then *Burnewin* comes on like Death
     At ev'ry chap.

Nae mercy, then, for airn or steel;
The brawnie, banie, ploughman-chiel
Brings hard owrehip, wi' sturdy wheel,
     The strong forehammer,
Till block an' studdie ring an' reel
     Wi' dinsome clamour.

When skirlin weanies see the light,
Thou maks the gossips clatter bright,
How fumbling coofs their dearies slight,
     Wae worth them for't!
While healths gae round to him wha, *tight*,
     Gies famous sport.

When neebors anger at a plea,
An' just as wud as wud can be,
How easy can the *barley-brie*
     Cement the quarrel!
It's aye the cheapest Lawyer's fee
     To taste the barrel.

Alake! that e'er my *Muse* has reason,
To wyte her countrymen wi' treason!
But monie daily weet their weason
    Wi' liquors nice,
An' hardly, in a winter season,
      E'er spier her price.

Wae worth that *Brandy*, burnan trash!
Fell source o' monie a pain an' brash!
Twins monie a poor, doylt, druken hash
    O' half his days;
An' sends, beside, auld *Scotland's* cash
      To her warst faes.

Ye Scots wha wish auld Scotland well,
Ye chief, to you my tale I tell,
Poor, plackless devils like *mysel*,
    It sets you ill,
Wi' bitter, dearthfu' *wines* to mell,
      Or foreign gill.

May *Gravels* round his blather wrench,
An' *Gouts* torment him, inch by inch,
What twists his gruntle wi' a glunch
    O' sour disdain,
Out owre a glass o' *Whisky-punch*
      Wi' honest men!

O *Whisky!* soul o' plays an' pranks!
Accept a *Bardie's* gratefu' thanks!
When wanting thee, what tuneless cranks
    Are my poor Verses!
Thou comes – they rattle i' their ranks
      At ither's arses!

Thee *Ferintosh!* O sadly lost!
Scotland lament frae coast to coast!
Now colic-grips, an' barkin hoast,
      May kill us a';
For loyal Forbes' *Charter'd boast*
      Is ta'en awa!

Thae curst horse-leeches o' th' Excise,
Wha mak the *Whisky stells* their prize!
Haud up thy han' *Deil!* ance, twice, *thrice!*
      There, sieze the blinkers!
An' bake them up in brunstane pies
      For poor d—n'd *Drinkers*.

Fortune, if thou'll but gie me still
Hale breeks, a scone, an' *whisky gill*,
An' rowth o' *rhyme* to rave at will,
      Tak a' the rest,
An' deal't about as thy blind skill
      Directs thee best.

The Author's earnest cry and prayer, to the right honorable and honorable, the Scotch representatives in the House of Commons

Dearest of Distillation! last and best! —
— How art thou lost! —

PARODY ON MILTON

Ye *Irish lords*, ye *knights* an' *squires*,
Wha *represent* our *Brughs* an' *Shires*,
An' dousely manage our affairs
      In *Parliament*,
To you a simple Bardie's pray'rs
      Are humbly sent.

Alas! my roupet *Muse* is haerse!
Your Honor's hearts wi' grief 'twad pierce,
To see her sittan on her arse
      Low i' the dust,
An' scriechan out prosaic verse,
      An' like to brust!

Tell them wha hae the chief direction,
Scotland an' *me's* in great affliction,
E'er sin' they laid that curst restriction
      On Aquavitæ;
An' rouse them up to strong conviction,
      An' move their pity.

Stand forth and tell yon Premier Youth,
The honest, open, naked truth:
Tell him o' mine an' Scotland's drouth,
        His servants humble:
The muckle devil blaw you south,
        If ye dissemble!

Does ony *great man* glunch an' gloom?
Speak out an' never fash your thumb.
Let *posts* an' *pensions* sink or swoom
        Wi' them wha grant them:
If honestly they canna come,
        Far better want them.

In gath'rin votes you were na slack,
Now stand as tightly by your tack:
Ne'er claw your lug, an' fidge your back,
        An' hum an' haw,
But raise your arm, an' tell your crack
        Before them a'.

Paint Scotland greetan owre her thrissle;
Her *mutchkin stowp* as toom's a whissle;
An' d—mn'd Excise-men in a bussle,
        Seizan a *Stell*,
Triumphant crushan't like a muscle
        Or laimpet shell.

Then on the tither hand present her,
A blackguard *Smuggler*, right behint her,
An' cheek-for-chow, a chuffie *Vintner*,
        Colleaguing join,
Picking her pouch as bare as Winter,
        Of a' kind coin.

Is there, that bears the name o' Scot,
But feels his heart's bluid rising hot,
To see his poor, auld Mither's *pot*,
   Thus dung in staves,
An' plunder'd o' her hindmost groat,
   By gallows knaves?

Alas! I'm but a nameless wight,
Trode i' the mire out o' sight!
But could I like Montgomeries fight,
   Or gab like Boswell,
There's some *sark-necks* I wad *draw* tight,
   An' *tye* some *hose* well.

God bless your Honors, can ye see't,
The kind, auld, cantie Carlin greet,
An' no get warmly to your feet,
   An' gar them hear it,
An' tell them, wi' a patriot-heat,
   Ye winna bear it?

Some o' you nicely ken the laws,
To round the period an' pause,
An' with rhetoric clause on clause
   To mak harangues;
Then echo thro' Saint Stephen's wa's
   Auld Scotland's wrangs.

Dempster, a true-blue Scot I'se warran;
Thee, aith-detesting, chaste *Kilkerran*;
An' that glib-gabbet Highland Baron,
   The Laird o' *Graham*;
And ane, a chap that's d—mn'd auldfarran,
   Dundas his name.

Erskine, a spunkie norland billie;
True Campbells, *Frederick* an' *Ilay*;
An' Livistone, the bauld *Sir Willie*;
      An' monie ithers,
Whom auld Demosthenes or Tully
      Might own for brithers.

  Arouse my boys! exert your mettle,
To get auld Scotland back her *kettle!*
Or faith! I'll wad my new pleugh-pettle,
      Ye'll see't or lang,
She'll teach you, wi' a reekan whittle,
      Anither sang.

  This while she's been in crankous mood,
Her *lost Militia* fir'd her bluid;
(Deil na they never mair do guid,
      Play'd her that pliskie!)
An' now she's like to rin red-wud
      About her *Whisky*.

  An' L—d! if ance they pit her till't,
Her tartan petticoat she'll kilt,
An' durk an' pistol at her belt,
      She'll tak the streets,
An' rin her whittle to the hilt,
      I' th' first she meets!

  For G—d-sake, Sirs! then speak her fair,
An' straik her cannie wi' the hair,
An' to the *muckle house* repair,
      Wi' instant speed,
An' strive, wi' a' your Wit an' Lear,
      To get remead.

Yon ill-tongu'd tinkler, *Charlie Fox*,
May taunt you wi' his jeers an' mocks;
But gie him't het, my hearty cocks!
　　　　E'en cowe the cadie!
An' send him to his dicing box,
　　　　An' sportin lady.

Tell yon guid bluid o' auld *Boconnock's*,
I'll be his debt twa mashlum bonnocks,
An' drink his health in auld *Nanse Tinnock's* *
　　　　Nine times a week,
If he some scheme, like tea an' winnocks,
　　　　Wad kindly seek.

Could he some *commutation* broach,
I'll pledge my aith in guid braid Scotch,
He need na fear their foul reproach
　　　　Nor erudition,
Yon mixtie-maxtie, queer hotch-potch,
　　　　The *Coalition*.

Auld Scotland has a raucle tongue;
She's just a devil wi' a rung;
An' if she promise auld or young
　　　　To tak their part,
Tho' by the neck she should be strung,
　　　　She'll no desert.

* A worthy old Hostess of the Author's in *Mauchline*, where he sometimes
studies Politics over a glass of guid, auld *Scotch Drink*.

And now, ye chosen five and forty,
May still your Mither's heart support ye;
Then, tho' a *Minister* grow dorty,
        An' kick your place,
Ye'll snap your fingers, poor an' hearty,
        Before his face.

God bless your Honors, a' your days,
Wi' sowps o' kail and brats o' claise,
In spite o' a' the thievish kaes
        That haunt St *Jamie's!*
Your humble Bardie sings an' prays
        While *Rab* his name is.

POSTSCRIPT

Let half-starv'd slaves in warmer skies,
See future wines, rich-clust'ring, rise;
Their lot auld Scotland ne'er envies,
        But blythe an' frisky,
She eyes her freeborn, martial boys,
        Tak aff their Whisky.

What tho' their Phœbus kinder warms,
While Fragrance blooms an' Beauty charms!
When wretches range, in famish'd swarms,
        The scented groves,
Or hounded forth, *dishonor* arms
        In hungry droves.

Their *gun's* a burden on their shouther;
They downa bide the stink o' *powther*;
Their bauldest thought's a hank'ring swither,
        To stan' or rin,
Till skelp – a shot – they're aff, a' throw'ther,
        To save their skin.

But bring a Scotchman frae his hill,
Clap in his cheek a *Highland gill,*
Say, such is royal George's will,
      An' there's the foe,
He has nae thought but how to kill
      Twa at a blow.

    Nae cauld, faint-hearted doubtings tease him;
Death comes, wi' fearless eye he sees him;
Wi' bluidy han' a welcome gies him;
      An' when he fa's,
His latest draught o' breathin lea'es him
      In faint huzzas.

    Sages their solemn een may steek,
An' raise a philosophic reek,
An' physically causes seek,
      In *clime* an' *season,*
But tell me *Whisky's* name in Greek,
      I'll tell the reason.

    Scotland, my auld, respected Mither!
Tho' whyles ye moistify your leather,
Till whare ye sit, on craps o' heather,
      Ye tine your dam;
Freedom and Whisky gang thegither,
      Tak aff your *dram!*

The Holy Fair

A robe of seeming truth and trust
Hid crafty observation;
And secret hung, with poison'd crust,
The dirk of Defamation:
A mask that like the gorget show'd,
Dye-varying, on the pigeon;
And for a mantle large and broad,
He wrapt him in Religion.

HYPOCRISY À-LA-MODE

I

Upon a simmer Sunday morn,
  When Nature's face is fair,
I walked forth to view the corn,
  An' snuff the callor air.
The rising sun, our Galston Muirs,
  Wi' glorious light was glintan;
The hares were hirplan down the furrs,
  The lav'rocks they were chantan
        Fu' sweet that day.

II

As lightsomely I glowr'd abroad,
  To see a scene sae gay,
Three *hizzies*, early at the road,
  Cam skelpan up the way.
Twa had manteeles o' dolefu' black,
  But ane wi' lyart lining;
The third, that gaed a wee a-back,
  Was in the fashion shining
        Fu' gay that day.

III

The *twa* appear'd like sisters twin,
  In feature, form an' claes;
Their visage wither'd, lang an' thin,
  An' sour as ony slaes:
The *third* cam up, hap-step-an'-loup,
  As light as ony lambie,
An' wi' a curchie low did stoop,
  As soon as e'er she saw me,
      Fu' kind that day.

IV

Wi' bonnet aff, quoth I, 'Sweet lass,
  I think ye seem to ken me;
I'm sure I've seen that bonie face,
  But yet I canna name ye.'
Quo' she, an' laughan as she spak,
  An' taks me by the han's,
'Ye, for my sake, hae gien the feck
  Of a' the *ten comman's*
      A screed some day.'

V

'My name is Fun – your cronie dear,
  The nearest friend ye hae;
An' this is Superstition here,
  An' that's Hypocrisy.
I'm gaun to ******** *holy fair*,
  To spend an hour in daffin:
Gin ye'll go there, yon runkl'd pair,
  We will get famous laughin
      At them this day.'

VI

Quoth I, 'With a' my heart, I'll do't;
    I'll get my sunday's sark on,
An' meet you on the holy spot;
    Faith, we'se hae fine remarkin!'
Then I gaed hame at crowdie-time,
    An' soon I made me ready;
For roads were clad, frae side to side,
    Wi' monie a wearie body,
            In droves that day.

VII

Here, farmers gash, in ridin graith,
    Gaed hoddan by their cotters;
There, swankies young, in braw braid-claith,
    Are springan owre the gutters.
The lasses, skelpan barefit, thrang,
    In silks an' scarlets glitter;
Wi' *sweet-milk cheese*, in monie a whang,
    An' *farls*, bak'd wi' butter,
            Fu' crump that day.

VIII

When by the *plate* we set our nose,
    Weel heaped up wi' ha'pence,
A greedy glowr *black-bonnet* throws,
    An' we maun draw our tippence.
Then in we go to see the show,
    On ev'ry side they're gath'ran;
Some carryan dails, some chairs an' stools,
    An' some are busy bleth'ran
            Right loud that day.

IX

Here stands a shed to fend the show'rs,
 An' screen our countra Gentry;
There, *racer Jess*, an' twathree wh——res,
 Are blinkan at the entry.
Here sits a raw o' tittlan jads,
 Wi' heaving breasts an' bare neck;
An' there, a batch o' *Wabster lads*,
 Blackguarding frae K*******ck
 For *fun* this day.

X

Here, some are thinkan on their sins,
 An' some upo' their claes;
Ane curses feet that fyl'd his shins,
 Anither sighs an' prays:
On this hand sits an *Elect* swatch,
 Wi' screw'd-up, grace-proud faces;
On that, a set o' chaps, at watch,
 Thrang winkan on the lasses
 To *chairs* that day.

XI

O happy is that man, an' blest!
 Nae wonder that it pride him!
Whase ain dear lass, that he likes best,
 Comes clinkan down beside him!
Wi' arm repos'd on the *chair-back*,
 He sweetly does compose him;
Which, by degrees, slips round her *neck*,
 An's loof upon her *bosom*
 Unkend that day.

XII

Now a' the congregation o'er
   Is silent expectation;
For ****** speels the holy door,
   Wi' tidings o' s—lv—t—n.
Should *Hornie*, as in ancient days,
   'Mang sons o' G— present him,
The vera sight o' ******'s face,
   To's ain *het hame* had sent him
      Wi' fright that day.

XIII

Hear how he clears the points o' Faith
   Wi' rattlin an' thumpin!
Now meekly calm, now wild in wrath,
   He's stampan, an' he's jumpan!
His lengthen'd chin, his turn'd up snout,
   His eldritch squeel an' gestures,
O how they fire the heart devout,
   Like *cantharidian* plaisters
      On sic a day!

XIV

But hark! the *tent* has chang'd it's voice;
   There's peace an' rest nae langer;
For a' the *real judges* rise,
   They canna sit for anger.
***** opens out his cauld harangues,
   On *practice* and on *morals*;
An' aff the *godly* pour in thrangs,
   To gie the jars an' barrels
      A lift that day.

XV

What signifies his barren shine,
  Of *moral pow'rs* an' *reason?*
His English style, an' gesture fine,
  Are a' clean out o' season.
Like Socrates or Antonine,
  Or some auld pagan heathen,
The *moral man* he does define,
  But ne'er a word o' *faith* in
      That's right that day.

XVI

In guid time comes an antidote
  Against sic poosion'd nostrum;
For *******, frae the water-fit,
  Ascends the *holy rostrum*:
See, up he's got the word o' G—,
  An' meek an' mim has view'd it,
While Common-sense has taen the road,
  An' aff, an' up the *Cowgate*
      Fast, fast that day.

XVII

Wee ****** niest, the Guard relieves,
  An' Orthodoxy raibles,
Tho' in his heart he weel believes,
  An' thinks it auld wives' fables:
But faith! the birkie wants a *Manse*,
  So, cannilie he hums them;
Altho' his *carnal* Wit an' Sense
  Like hafflins-wise o'ercomes him
      At times that day.

XVIII

Now, butt an' ben, the Change-house fills,
   Wi' *yill-caup* Commentators:
Here's crying out for bakes an' gills,
   An' there the pint-stowp clatters;
While thick an' thrang, an' loud an' lang;
   Wi' *Logic*, an' wi' *Scripture*,
They raise a din, that, in the end,
   Is like to breed a rupture
          O' wrath that day.

XIX

Leeze me on Drink! it gies us mair
   Than either School or Colledge:
It kindles Wit, it waukens Lear,
   It pangs us fou o' Knowledge.
Be't *whisky-gill* or *penny-wheep*,
   Or ony stronger potion,
It never fails, on drinkin deep,
   To kittle up our *notion*,
          By night or day.

XX

The lads an' lasses, blythely bent
   To mind baith *saul* an' *body*,
Sit round the table, weel content,
   An' steer about the *toddy*.
On this ane's dress, an' that ane's lcuk,
   They're makin observations;
While some are cozie i' the neuk,
   An' forming *assignations*
          To meet some day.

XXI

But now the L—'s ain trumpet touts,
    Till a' the hills are rairan,
An' echos back return the shouts;
    Black ****** is na spairan:
His piercin words, like Highlan swords,
    Divide the joints an' marrow;
His talk o' H—ll, whare devils dwell,
    Our vera 'Sauls does harrow'*
          Wi' fright that day!

XXII

A vast, unbottom'd, boundless *Pit*,
    Fill'd fou o' *lowan brunstane*,
Whase raging flame, an' scorching heat,
    Wad melt the hardest whun-stane!
The *half asleep* start up wi' fear,
    An' think they hear it roaran,
When presently it does appear,
    'Twas but some neebor *snoran*
          Asleep that day.

XXIII

'Twad be owre lang a tale to tell,
    How monie stories past,
An' how they crouded to the yill,
    When they were a' dismist:
How drink gaed round, in cogs an' caups,
    Amang the furms an' benches;
An' *cheese* an' *bread*, frae women's laps,
    Was dealt about in lunches,
          An' dawds that day.

---

* Shakespeare's *Hamlet*.

XXIV

In comes a gawsie, gash *Guidwife*,
   An' sits down by the fire,
Syne draws her *kebbuck* an' her knife;
   The lasses they are shyer.
The auld *Guidmen*, about the *grace*,
   Frae side to side they bother,
Till some ane by his bonnet lays,
   An' gies them't, like a *tether*,
         Fu' lang that day.

XXV

Waesucks! for him that gets nae lass,
   Or lasses that hae naething!
Sma' need has he to say a grace,
   Or melvie his braw claithing!
O *Wives* be mindfu', ance yoursel,
   How bonie lads ye wanted,
An' dinna, for a *kebbuck-heel*,
   Let lasses be affronted
         On sic a day!

XXVI

Now *Clinkumbell*, wi' rattlan tow,
   Begins to jow an' croon;
Some swagger hame, the best they dow,
   Some wait the afternoon.
At slaps the billies halt a blink,
   Till lasses strip their shoon:
Wi' *faith* an' *hope*, an' *love* an' *drink*,
   They're a' in famous tune
         For crack that day.

XXVII

How monie hearts this day converts,
  O' sinners and o' Lasses!
Their hearts o' stane, gin night are gane,
  As saft as ony flesh is.
There's some are fou o' *love divine*;
  There's some are fou o' *brandy*;
An' monie jobs that day begin,
  May end in *Houghmagandie*
      Some ither day.

Address to the Deil

O Prince, O chief of many throned pow'rs,
That led th'embattl'd Seraphim to war –

MILTON

O Thou, whatever title suit thee!
Auld Hornie, Satan, Nick, or Clootie,
Wha in yon cavern grim an' sootie,
      Clos'd under hatches,
Spairges about the brunstane cootie,
      To scaud poor wretches!

Hear me, *auld Hangie*, for a wee,
An' let poor, *damned bodies* bee;
I'm sure sma' pleasure it can gie,
      Ev'n to a *deil*,
To skelp an' scaud poor dogs like me,
      An' hear us squeel!

Great is thy pow'r, an' great thy fame;
Far kend an' noted is thy name;
An' tho' yon *lowan heugh's* thy hame,
      Thou travels far;
An' faith! thou's neither lag nor lame,
      Nor blate nor scaur.

Whyles, ranging like a roaran lion,
For prey, a' holes an' corners tryin;
Whyles, on the strong-wing'd Tempest flyin,
      Tirlan the *kirks*;
Whyles, in the human bosom pryin,
      Unseen thou lurks.

I've heard my rev'rend *Graunie* say,
In lanely glens ye like to stray;
Or where auld, ruin'd castles, gray,
   Nod to the moon,
Ye fright the nightly wand'rer's way,
    Wi' eldritch croon.

 When twilight did my *Graunie* summon,
To say her pray'rs, douse, honest woman!
Aft 'yont the dyke she's heard you bumman,
   Wi' eerie drone;
Or, rustling, thro' the boortries coman,
    Wi' heavy groan.

 Ae dreary, windy, winter night,
The stars shot down wi' sklentan light,
Wi' you, *mysel*, I gat a fright,
   Ayont the lough;
Ye, like a *rash-buss*, stood in sight,
    Wi' waving sugh.

 The cudgel in my nieve did shake,
Each bristl'd hair stood like a stake,
When wi' an eldritch, stoor *quaick, quaick,*
   Amang the springs.
Awa ye squatter'd like a *drake*,
    On whistling wings.

 Let *Warlocks* grim, an' wither'd *Hags*,
Tell how wi' you on ragweed nags,
They skim the muirs an' dizzy crags,
   Wi' wicked speed;
And in kirk-yards renew their leagues,
    Owre howcket dead.

Thence, countra wives, wi' toil an' pain,
May plunge an' plunge the *kirn* in vain;
For Oh! the yellow treasure's taen
      By witching skill;
An' dawtet, twal-pint *Hawkie's* gane
      As yell's the Bill.

Thence, mystic knots mak great abuse,
On *Young-Guidmen*, fond, keen an' croose;
When the best *wark-lume* i' the house,
      By cantraip wit,
Is instant made no worth a louse,
      Just at the bit.

When thowes dissolve the snawy hoord,
An' float the jinglan icy boord,
Then, *Water-kelpies* haunt the foord,
      By your direction,
An' nighted Trav'llers are allur'd
      To their destruction.

An' aft your moss-traversing *Spunkies*
Decoy the wight that late an' drunk is:
The bleezan, curst, mischievous monkies
      Delude his eyes,
Till in some miry slough he sunk is,
      Ne'er mair to rise.

When Masons' mystic *word* an' *grip*,
In storms an' tempests raise you up,
Some cock or cat, your rage maun stop,
      Or, strange to tell!
The *youngest Brother* ye wad whip
      Aff straught to *H—ll*.

Lang syne in Eden's bonie yard,
When youthfu' lovers first were pair'd,
An' all the Soul of Love they shar'd,
   The raptur'd hour,
Sweet on the fragrant, flow'ry swaird,
   In shady bow'r.

 Then you, ye auld, snick-drawing dog!
Ye cam to Paradise incog,
An' play'd on man a cursed brogue,
   (Black be your fa'!)
An' gied the infant warld a shog,
   'Maist ruin'd a'.

 D'ye mind that day, when in a bizz,
Wi' reeket duds, an' reestet gizz,
Ye did present your smoutie phiz,
   'Mang better folk,
An' sklented on the *man of Uzz*,
   Your spitefu' joke?

 An how ye gat him i' your thrall,
An' brak him out o' house an' hal',
While scabs an' botches did him gall,
   Wi' bitter claw,
An' lows'd his ill-tongu'd, wicked *Scawl*
   Was warst ava?

But a' your doings to rehearse,
Your wily snares an' fechtin fierce,
Sin' that day Michael* did you pierce,
    Down to this time,
Wad ding a' *Lallan* tongue, or *Erse*,
      In Prose or Rhyme.

An' now, auld *Cloots*, I ken ye're thinkan,
A certain *Bardie's* rantin, drinkin,
Some luckless hour will send him linkan,
    To your black pit;
But faith! he'll turn a corner jinkan,
      An' cheat you yet.

But fare-you-weel, auld *Nickie-ben*!
O wad ye tak a thought an' men'!
Ye aiblins might – I dinna ken –
    Still hae a *stake* –
I'm wae to think upo' yon den,
      Ev'n for your sake!

* *Vide* Milton, Book 6th.

The death and dying words of Poor Mailie the Author's only pet Yowe

AN UNCO MOURNFU' TALE

As Mailie, an' her lambs thegither,
Was ae day nibbling on the tether,
Upon her cloot she coost a hitch,
An' owre she warsl'd in the ditch:
There, groaning, dying, she did ly,
When *Hughoc** he cam doytan by.

Wi' glowrin een, an' lifted han's,
Poor *Hughoc* like a statue stan's;
He saw her days were near hand ended,
But, waes my heart! he could na mend it!
He gaped wide, but naething spak,
At length poor *Mailie* silence brak.

'O thou, whase lamentable face
Appears to mourn my woefu' case!
My *dying words* attentive hear,
An' bear them to my *Master* dear.

Tell him, if e'er again he keep
As muckle gear as buy a *sheep*,
O, bid him never tye them mair,
Wi' wicked strings o' hemp or hair!

---

* A neibor herd-callan.

But ca them out to park or hill,
An' let them wander at their will:
So, may his flock increase an' grow
To *scores* o' lambs, an' *packs* of woo'!

Tell him, he was a Master kin',
An' ay was guid to me an' mine:
An' now my *dying* charge I gie him,
My helpless *lambs*, I trust them wi' him.

O, bid him save their harmless lives,
Frae dogs an' tods, an' butchers' knives!
But gie them guid *cow-milk* their fill,
Till they be fit to fend themsel;
An' tent them duely, e'en an' morn,
Wi' taets o' *hay* an' ripps o' *corn*.

An' may they never learn the gaets,
Of ither vile, wanrestfu' *Pets!*
To slink thro' slaps, an' reave an' steal,
At stacks o' pease, or stocks o' kail.
So may they, like their great *forbears*,
For monie a year come thro' the sheers:
So *wives* will gie them bits o' bread,
An' *bairns* greet for them when they're dead.

My poor *toop-lamb*, my son an' heir,
O, bid him breed him up wi' care!
An' if he live to be a beast,
To pit some havins in his breast!
An' warn him ay at ridin time,
To stay content wi' *yowes* at hame
An' no to rin an' wear his cloots,
Like ither menseless, graceless brutes.

An' niest my *yowie*, silly thing,
Gude keep thee frae a *tether string!*
O, may thou ne'er forgather up,
Wi' onie blastet, moorlan *toop*;
But ay keep mind to moop an' mell,
Wi' sheep o' credit like thysel!

And now, *my bairns*, wi' my last breath,
I lea'e my blessin wi' you baith:
An' when ye think upo' your Mither,
Mind to be kind to ane anither.

Now, honest Hughoc, dinna fail,
To tell my Master a' my tale;
An' bid him burn this cursed *tether*,
An' for thy pains thou'se get my blather.'

This said, poor *Mailie* turn'd her head,
An' clos'd her een amang the dead!

POOR MAILIE'S ELEGY

Lament in rhyme, lament in prose,
Wi' saut tears trickling down your nose;
Our *Bardie's* fate is at a close,
     Past a' remead!
The last, sad cape-stane of his woes;
     Poor Mailie's dead!

It's no the loss o' warl's gear,
That could sae bitter draw the tear,
Or make our *Bardie*, dowie, wear
     The mourning weed:
He's lost a friend and neebor dear,
     In *Mailie* dead.

Thro' a' the town she trotted by him;
A lang half-mile she could descry him;
Wi' kindly bleat, when she did spy him,
      She ran wi' speed:
A friend mair faithfu' ne'er came nigh him,
      Than *Mailie* dead.

I wat she was a *sheep* o' sense,
An' could behave hersel wi' mense:
I'll say't, she never brak a fence,
      Thro' thievish greed,
Our *Bardie*, lanely, keeps the spence
      Sin' *Mailie's* dead.

Or, if he wanders up the howe,
Her living image in *her yowe*,
Comes bleating till him, owre the knowe,
      For bits o' bread;
An' down the briny pearls rowe
      For *Mailie* dead.

She was nae get o' moorlan tips,
Wi' tauted ket, an' hairy hips;
For her forbears were brought in ships,
      Frae 'yont the Tweed:
A bonier *fleesh* ne'er cross'd the clips
      Than *Mailie's* dead.

Wae worth that man wha first did shape.
That vile, wanchancie thing – *a raep!*
It maks guid fellows girn an' gape,
      Wi' chokin dread;
An' *Robin's* bonnet wave wi' crape
      For *Mailie* dead.

O, a' ye *Bards* on bonie Doon!
An' wha on Aire your chanters tune!
Come, join the melancholious croon
      O' *Robin's* reed!
His heart will never get aboon!
      His *Mailie's* dead!

*To J. S*****

Friendship, mysterious cement of the soul!
Sweet'ner of Life, and solder of Society!
I owe thee much——

BLAIR

Dear S****, the sleest, pawkie thief,
That e'er attempted stealth or rief,
Ye surely hae some warlock-breef
      Owre human hearts;
For ne'er a bosom yet was prief
      Against your arts.

For me, I swear by sun an' moon,
And ev'ry star that blinks aboon,
Ye've cost me twenty pair o' shoon
      Just gaun to see you;
And ev'ry ither pair that's done,
      Mair taen I'm wi' you.

That auld, capricious carlin, *Nature*,
To mak amends for scrimpet stature,
She's turn'd you off, a human-creature
      On her *first* plan,
And in her freaks, on ev'ry feature,
      She's wrote, *the Man.*

Just now I've taen the fit o' rhyme,
My barmie noddle's working prime,
My fancy yerket up sublime
      Wi' hasty summon:
Hae ye a leisure-moment's time
      To hear what's comin?

Some rhyme a neebor's name to lash;
Some rhyme, (vain thought!) for needfu' cash;
Some rhyme to court the countra clash,
   An' raise a din;
For me, an *aim* I never fash;
   I rhyme for *fun*.

 The star that rules my luckless lot,
Has fated me the russet coat,
An' damn'd my fortune to the groat;
   But, in requit,
Has blest me with a *random-shot*
   O' countra wit.

 This while my notion's taen a sklent,
To try my fate in guid, black *prent*;
But still the mair I'm that way bent,
   Something cries, 'Hoolie!
I red you, honest man, tak tent!
   Ye'll shaw your folly.

 There's ither Poets, much your betters,
Far seen in *Greek*, deep men o' *letters*,
Hae thought they had ensur'd their debtors,
   A' future ages;
Now moths deform in shapeless tatters,
   Their unknown pages.'

 Then farewel hopes of Laurel-boughs,
To garland my poetic brows!
Henceforth, I'll rove where busy ploughs
   Are whistling thrang,
An' teach the lanely heights an' howes
   My rustic sang.

I'll wander on with tentless heed,
How never-halting moments speed,
Till fate shall snap the brittle thread;
          Then, all unknown,
I'll lay me with th' *inglorious dead*,
          Forgot and gone!

But why, o' Death, begin a tale?
Just now we're living sound an' hale;
Then top and maintop croud the sail,
          Heave *Care* o'er-side!
And large, before Enjoyment's gale,
          Let's tak the tide.

This life, sae far's I understand,
Is a' enchanted fairy-land,
Where Pleasure is the Magic-wand,
          That, wielded right,
Maks Hours like Minutes, hand in hand,
          Dance by fu' light.

The *magic-wand* then let us wield;
For, ance that five an' forty's speel'd,
See, crazy, weary, joyless Eild,
          Wi' wrinkl'd face,
Comes hostan, hirplan owre the field,
          Wi' creeping pace.

When ance *life's day* draws near the gloamin,
Then fareweel vacant, careless roamin;
An' fareweel chearfu' tankards foamin,
          An' social noise;
An' fareweel dear, deluding woman,
          The joy of joys!

O *Life!* how pleasant in thy morning,
Young Fancy's rays the hills adorning!
Cold-pausing Caution's lesson scorning,
   We frisk away,
Like school-boys, at th' expected warning,
    To joy and play.

 We wander there, we wander here,
We eye the *rose* upon the brier,
Unmindful that the *thorn* is near,
   Among the leaves;
And tho' the puny wound appear,
    Short while it grieves.

 Some, lucky, find a flow'ry spot,
For which they never toil'd nor swat;
They drink the *sweet* and eat the *fat,*
   But care or pain;
And hap'ly, eye the barren hut,
    With high disdain.

 With steady aim, Some Fortune chase;
Keen hope does ev'ry sinew brace;
Thro' fair, thro' foul, they urge the race,
   And sieze the prey:
Then canie, in some cozie place,
    They close the *day.*

 And others, like your humble servan',
Poor wights! nae rules nor roads observin;
To right or left, eternal swervin,
   They zig-zag on;
Till curst with Age, obscure an' starvin,
    They aften groan.

Alas! what bitter toil an' straining –
But truce with peevish, poor complaining!
Is Fortune's fickle *Luna* waning?
  E'en let her gang!
Beneath what light she has remaining,
  Let's sing our Sang.

My pen I here fling to the door,
And kneel, 'Ye *Pow'rs*, and warm implore,
Tho' I should wander *Terra* o'er,
  In all her climes,
Grant me but this, I ask no more,
  Ay rowth o' rhymes.

Gie dreeping roasts to *countra Lairds*,
Till icicles hing frae their beards;
Gie fine braw claes to fine *Life-guards*,
  And *Maids of Honor*,
And yill an' whisky gie to *Cairds*,
  Until they sconner.

A *Title*, Dempster merits it;
A *Garter* gie to Willie Pit;
Gie Wealth to some be-ledger'd Cit,
  In cent per cent;
But give me real, sterling Wit,
  And I'm content.

While ye are pleas'd to keep me hale,
I'll sit down o'er my scanty meal,
Be't *water-brose*, or *muslin-kail*,
  Wi' chearfu' face,
As lang's the Muses dinna fail
  To say the grace.'

An anxious e'e I never throws
Behint my lug, or by my nose;
I jouk beneath Misfortune's blows
   As weel's I may;
Sworn foe to *sorrow*, *care*, and *prose*,
   I rhyme away.

 O ye, douse folk, that live by rule,
Grave, tideless-blooded, calm and cool,
Compar'd wi' you – O fool! fool! fool!
   How much unlike!
Your hearts are just a standing pool,
   Your lives, a dyke!

 Nae hare-brain'd, sentimental traces,
In your unletter'd, nameless faces!
In *arioso* trills and graces
   Ye never stray,
But *gravissimo*, solemn basses
   Ye hum away.

 Ye are sae *grave*, nae doubt ye're *wise*;
Nae ferly tho' ye do despise
The hairum-scairum, ram-stam boys,
   The rambling squad;
I see ye upward cast your eyes –
   – Ye ken the road –

 Whilst I – but I shall haud me there –
Wi' you I'll scarce gang *ony where* –
Then *Jamie*, I shall say nae mair,
   But quat my sang,
Content *with* you to make a *pair*,
   Whare'er I gang.

A Dream

Thoughts, words and deeds, the Statute blames with reason;
But surely Dreams *were ne'er indicted Treason.*

On reading, in the public papers, the
laureate's ode, with the other parade
of June 4th 1786, the author was no
sooner dropt asleep, than he imagined
himself transported to the birth-day
levee; and, in his dreaming fancy, made
the following address.

I

Guid-mornin to your Majesty!
　　May heaven augment your blisses,
On ev'ry new *Birth-day* ye see,
　　A humble Bardie wishes!
My Bardship here, at your Levee,
　　On sic a day as this is,
Is sure an uncouth sight to see,
　　Amang thae Birth-day dresses
　　　　　Sae fine this day.

II

I see ye're complimented thrang,
　　By many a *lord* an' *lady*;
'God save the King' 's a cukoo sang
　　That's unco easy said ay:
The *Poets* too, a venal gang,
　　Wi' rhymes weel-turn'd an' ready,
Wad gar you trow ye ne'er do wrang,
　　But ay unerring steady,
　　　　　On sic a day.

III

For me! before a Monarch's face,
  Ev'n *there* I winna flatter;
For neither Pension, Post, nor Place,
  Am I your humble debtor:
So, nae reflection on Your Grace,
  Your Kingship to bespatter;
There's monie *waur* been o' the Race,
  And aiblins *ane* been better
        Than You this day.

IV

'Tis very true, my sovereign King,
  My skill may weel be doubted;
But *Facts* are cheels that winna ding,
  An' downa be disputed:
Your *royal nest*, beneath *Your* wing,
  Is e'en right reft an' clouted,
And now the third part o' the string,
  An' less, will gang about it
        Than did ae day.

V

Far be't frae me that I aspire
  To blame your Legislation,
Or say, ye wisdom want, or fire,
  To rule this mighty nation;
But faith! I muckle doubt, my Sire,
  Ye've trusted 'Ministration,
To chaps, wha, in a *barn* or *byre*,
  Wad better fill'd their station
        Than *courts* yon day.

VI

And now Ye've gien auld *Britain* peace,
　　Her broken shins to plaister;
Your sair taxation does her fleece,
　　Till she has scarce a tester:
For me, thank God, my life's a *lease*,
　　Nae *bargain* wearing faster,
Or faith! I fear, that, wi' the geese,
　　I shortly boost to pasture
　　　　　　I' the craft some day.

VII

I'm no mistrusting *Willie Pit*,
　　When taxes he enlarges,
(An' *Will's* a true guid fallow's get,
　　A Name not Envy spairges)
That he intends to pay your *debt*,
　　An' lessen a' your *charges*;
But, G—d-sake! let nae *saving-fit*
　　Abridge your bonie *Barges*
　　　　　　An' *Boats* this day.

VIII

Adieu, my Liege! may Freedom geck
　　Beneath your high protection;
An' may Ye rax Corruption's neck,
　　And gie her for dissection!
But since I'm here, I'll no neglect,
　　In loyal, true affection,
To pay your Queen, with due respect,
　　My fealty an' subjection
　　　　　　This great Birth-day.

IX

Hail, *Majesty most Excellent!*
   While Nobles strive to please Ye,
Will Ye accept a Compliment,
   A simple Bardie gies Ye?
Thae bonie Bairntime, Heav'n has lent,
   Still higher may they heeze Ye
In bliss, till Fate some day is sent,
   For ever to release Ye
         Frae Care that day.

X

For you, young Potentate o' W—,
   I tell your *Highness* fairly,
Down Pleasure's stream, wi' swelling sails,
   I'm tauld ye're driving rarely;
But some day ye may gnaw your nails,
   An' curse your folly fairly,
That e'er ye brak Diana's *pales*,
   Or rattl'd dice wi' *Charlie*
         By night or day.

XI

Yet aft a ragged *Gowte's* been known,
   To mak a noble *Aiver*
So, ye may dousely fill a Throne,
   For a' their clish-ma-claver:
There, Him at *Agincourt* wha shone
   Few better were or braver;
And yet, wi' funny, queer *Sir John,**
   He was an unco shaver
         For monie a day.

* Sir John Falstaff, *Vide* Shakespeare.

XII

For you, right rev'rend O———,
    Nane sets the *lawn-sleeve* sweeter,
Altho' a ribban at your lug
    Wad been a dress compleater:
As ye disown yon paughty dog,
    That *bears* the Keys of Peter,
Then swith! an' get a *wife* to hug,
    Or trouth! ye'll stain the *Mitre*
            Some luckless day.

XIII

Young, royal Tarry-Breeks, I learn,
    Ye've lately come athwart her;
A glorious *Galley*,* stem and stern,
    Weel rigg'd for *Venus barter*;
But first hang out that she'll discern
    Your *hymeneal Charter*,
Then heave aboard your *grapple airn*,
    An', large upon her *quarter*,
            Come full that day.

XIV

Ye lastly, bonie blossoms a',
    Ye *royal Lasses* dainty,
Heav'n mak you guid as weel as braw,
    An' gie you *lads* a plenty:
But sneer na *British-boys* awa;
    For King's are unco scant ay,
An' German-Gentles are but *sma'*,
    They're better just than *want ay*
            On onie day.

* Alluding to the Newspaper account of a certain royal Sailor's Amour.

XV

God bless you a'! consider now,
    Ye're unco muckle dautet;
But ere the *course* o' life be through,
    It may be bitter sautet:
An' I hae seen their *coggie* fou,
    That yet hae tarrow't at it,
But or the *day* was done, I trow,
    The laggen they hae clautet
        Fu' clean that day.

The Vision

DUAN FIRST*

The sun had clos'd the *winter-day*,
The Curlers quat their roaring play,
And hunger'd Maukin taen her way
    To kail-yards green,
While faithless snaws ilk step betray
    Whare she has been.

The Thresher's weary *flingin-tree*,
The lee-lang day had tir'd me;
And when the Day had clos'd his e'e,
    Far i' the West,
Ben i' the *Spence*, right pensivelie,
    I gaed to rest.

There, lanely, by the ingle-cheek,
I sat and ey'd the spewing reek,
That fill'd, wi' hoast-provoking smeek,
    The auld, clay biggin;
And heard the restless rattons squeak
    About the riggin.

All in this mottie, misty clime,
I backward mus'd on wasted time,
How I had spent my *youthfu' prime*,
    An' done nae-thing,
But stringing blethers up in rhyme
    For fools to sing.

* Duan, a term of Ossian's for the different divisions of a digressive Poem.
See his *Cath Loda*, Vol. 2 of McPherson's Translation.

Had I to guid advice but harket,
I might, by this, hae led a market,
Or strutted in a Bank and clarket
      My *Cash-Account,*
While here, half-mad, half-fed, half-sarket,
      Is a' th' amount.

  I started, mutt'ring blockhead! coof!
And heav'd on high my wauket loof,
To swear by a' yon starry roof,
      Or some rash aith,
That I, henceforth, would be *rhyme-proof*
      Till my last breath –

  When click! the *string* the *snick* did draw;
And jee! the door gaed to the wa';
And by my ingle-lowe I saw,
      Now bleezan bright,
A tight, outlandish *Hizzie*, braw,
      Come full in sight.

  Ye need na doubt, I held my whisht;
The infant aith, half-form'd, was crusht;
I glowr'd as eerie's I'd been dusht,
      In some wild glen;
When sweet, like *modest Worth*, she blusht,
      And stepped ben.

  Green, slender, leaf-clad *Holly-boughs*
Were twisted, gracefu', round her brows,
I took her for some Scottish Muse,
      By that same token;
And come to stop those reckless vows,
      Would soon been broken.

A 'hare-brain'd, sentimental trace'
Was strongly marked in her face;
A wildly-witty, rustic grace
   Shone full upon her;
Her *eye*, ev'n turn'd on empty space,
   Beam'd keen with *Honor*.

Down flow'd her robe, a *tartan* sheen,
Till half a leg was scrimply seen;
And such a *leg!* my Bess, I ween,
   Could only peer it;
Sae straught, sae taper, tight and clean,
   Nane else came near it.

Her *Mantle* large, of greenish hue,
My gazing wonder chiefly drew;
Deep *lights* and *shades*, bold-mingling, threw
   A lustre grand;
And seem'd, to my astonish'd view,
   A *well-known* Land.

Here, rivers in the sea were lost;
There, mountains to the skies were tost:
Here, tumbling billows mark'd the coast,
   With surging foam;
There, distant shone, *Art's* lofty boast,
   The lordly dome.

Here, Doon pour'd down his far-fetch'd floods;
There, well-fed Irwine stately thuds:
Auld, hermit Aire staw thro' his woods,
   On to the shore;
And many a lesser torrent scuds,
   With seeming roar.

Low, in a sandy valley spread,
An ancient Borough rear'd her head;
Still, as in *Scottish Story* read,
   She boasts a *Race*,
To ev'ry nobler virtue bred,
   And polish'd grace.

DUAN SECOND

With musing-deep, astonish'd stare,
I view'd the heavenly-seeming *Fair*;
A whisp'ring *throb* did witness bear
   Of kindred sweet,
When with an elder Sister's air
   She did me greet.

'All hail! *my own* inspired Bard!
In me thy native Muse regard!
Nor longer mourn thy fate is hard,
   Thus poorly low!
I come to give thee such *reward*,
   As *we* bestow.

Know, the great *Genius* of this Land,
Has many a light, aerial band,
Who, all beneath his high command,
   Harmoniously,
As *Arts* or *Arms* they understand,
   Their labors ply.

They Scotia's Race among them share;
Some fire the *Sodger* on to dare;
Some rouse the *Patriot* up to bare
      Corruption's heart:
Some teach the *Bard*, a darling care,
      The tuneful Art.

'Mong swelling floods of reeking gore,
They ardent, kindling spirits pour;
Or, mid the venal Senate's roar,
      They, fightless, stand,
To mend the honest *Patriot-lore*,
      And grace the hand.

Hence, Fullarton, the brave and young;
Hence, Dempster's truth-prevailing tongue;
Hence, sweet harmonious Beattie sung
      His "Minstrel lays";
Or tore, with noble ardour stung,
      The *Sceptic's* bays.

To lower Orders are assign'd,
The humbler ranks of Human kind,
The rustic Bard, the lab'ring Hind,
      The Artisan;
All chuse, as, various they're inclin'd,
      The various man.

When yellow waves the heavy grain,
The threat'ning *Storm*, some, strongly, rein;
Some teach to meliorate the plain,
      With *tillage-skill*;
And some instruct the Shepherd-train,
      Blythe o'er the hill.

Some hint the Lover's harmless wile;
Some grace the Maiden's artless smile;
Some soothe the Lab'rer's weary toil,
      For humble gains,
And make his *cottage scenes* beguile
      His cares and pains.

Some, bounded to a district-space,
Explore at large Man's *infant race*,
To mark the embryotic trace,
      Of *rustic Bard*;
And careful note each op'ning grace,
      A guide and guard.

Of these am I – Coila my name;
And this district as mine I claim,
Where once the *Campbells*, chiefs of fame,
      Held ruling pow'r:
I mark'd thy embryo-tuneful flame,
      Thy natal hour.

With future hope, I oft would gaze,
Fond, on thy little, early ways,
Thy rudely-caroll'd, chiming phrase,
      In uncouth rhymes,
Fir'd at the simple, artless lays
      Of other times.

I saw thee seek the sounding shore,
Delighted with the dashing roar;
Or when the *North* his fleecy store
      Drove thro' the sky,
I saw grim Nature's visage hoar,
      Struck thy young eye.

Or when the deep-green-mantl'd Earth,
Warm-cherish'd ev'ry floweret's birth,
And joy and music pouring forth,
   In ev'ry grove,
I saw thee eye the gen'ral mirth
    With boundless love.

When ripen'd fields, and azure skies,
Call'd forth the *Reaper's* rustling noise,
I saw thee leave their ev'ning joys,
   And lonely stalk,
To vent thy bosom's swelling rise,
    In pensive walk.

When *youthful Love*, warm-blushing, strong,
Keen-shivering shot thy nerves along,
Those accents, grateful to thy tongue,
   Th' adored *Name*,
I taught thee how to pour in song,
    To soothe thy flame.

I saw thy pulse's maddening play,
Wild-send thee Pleasure's devious way,
Misled by Fancy's *meteor-ray*,
   By Passion driven;
But yet the *light* that led astray,
    Was *light* from Heaven.

I taught thy manners-painting strains,
The *loves*, the *ways* of simple swains,
Till now, o'er all my wide domains,
   Thy fame extends;
And some, the pride of *Coila's* plains,
    Become thy friends.

Thou canst not learn, nor I can show,
To paint with *Thomson's* landscape-glow;
Or wake the bosom-melting throe,
   With *Shenstone's* art;
Or pour, with *Gray*, the moving flow,
   Warm on the heart.

 Yet all beneath th'unrivall'd Rose,
The lowly Daisy sweetly blows;
Tho' large the forest's Monarch throws
   His army shade,
Yet green the juicy Hawthorn grows,
   Adown the glade.

 Then never murmur nor repine;
Strive in thy *humble sphere* to shine;
And trust me, not *Potosi's mine*,
   Nor *King's regard*,
Can give a bliss o'ermatching thine,
   A *rustic Bard*.

 To give my counsels all in one,
Thy *tuneful flame* still careful fan;
Preserve *the dignity of Man*,
   With soul erect;
And trust, the Universal Plan
   Will all protect.

 And wear thou this' – She solemn said,
And bound the *Holly* round my head;
The polish'd leaves, and berries red,
   Did rustling play;
And, like a passing thought, she fled,
   In light away.

The following poem will, by many Readers, be well enough understood; but, for the sake of those who are unacquainted with the manners and traditions of the country where the scene is cast, Notes are added, to give some account of the principal Charms and Spells of that Night, so big with Prophecy to the Peasantry in the West of Scotland. The passion of prying into Futurity makes a striking part of the history of Human-nature, in its rude state, in all ages and nations; and it may be some entertainment to a philosophic mind, if any such should honor the Author with a perusal, to see the remains of it, among the more unenlightened in our own.

Halloween*

Yes! let the Rich deride, the Proud disdain,
The simple pleasures of the lowly train;
To me more dear, congenial to my heart,
One native charm, than all the gloss of art.

GOLDSMITH

I

Upon that *night*, when Fairies light,
   On *Cassilis Downans*† dance,
Or owre the lays, in splendid blaze,
   On sprightly coursers prance;
Or for *Colean*, the rout is taen,
   Beneath the moon's pale beams;
There, up the *Cove*,‡ to stray an' rove,
   Amang the rocks an' streams
          To sport that night.

II

Amang the bonie, winding banks,
   Where *Doon* rins, wimplin, clear,
Where Bruce¶ ance rul'd the martial ranks,
   An' shook his *Carrick* spear,

---

* Is thought to be a night when Witches, Devils, and other mischief-making beings, are all abroad on their baneful, midnight errands: particularly, those aerial people, the Fairies, are said, on that night, to hold a grand Anniversary.
† Certain little romantic, rocky, green hills, in the neighbourhood of the ancient seat of the Earls of Cassilis.
‡ A noted cavern near Colean house, called the Cove of Colean; which, as well as Cassilis Downans, is famed, in country story, for being a favourite haunt of Fairies.
¶ The famous family of that name, the ancestors of Robert the great Deliverer of his country, were Earls of Carrick.

Some merry, friendly, countra folks,
　　Together did convene,
To *burn* their nits, an' *pou* their stocks,
　　An' haud their *Halloween*
　　　　　Fu' blythe that night.

III

The lasses feat, an' cleanly neat,
　　Mair braw than when they're fine;
Their faces blythe, fu' sweetly kythe,
　　Hearts leal, an' warm, an' kin':
The lads sae trig, wi' wooer-babs,
　　Weel knotted on their garten,
Some unco blate, an' some wi' gabs,
　　Gar lasses hearts gang startin
　　　　　Whyles fast at night.

IV

Then, first an' foremost, thro' the kail,
　　Their *stocks** maun a' be sought ance;
They steek their een, an' grape an' wale,
　　For muckle anes, an' straught anes.
Poor hav'rel *Will* fell aff the drift,
　　An' wander'd thro' the *Bow-kail*,

* The first ceremony of Halloween, is, pulling each a *Stock*, or plant of kail.
They must go out, hand in hand, with eyes shut, and pull the first they meet
with: its being big or little, straight or crooked, is prophetic of the size and
shape of the grand object of all their Spells – the husband or wife. If any *yird*,
or earth, stick to the root, that is *tocher*, or fortune; and the taste of the *custoc*,
that is, the heart of the stem, is indicative of the natural temper and disposition.
Lastly, the stems, or to give them their ordinary appellation, the *runts*, are
placed somewhere above the head of the door; and the christian names of
the people whom chance brings into the house, are, according to the priority
of placing the *runts*, the names in question.

An' pow't, for want o' better shift,
　　A *runt* was like a sow-tail
　　　　Sae bow't that night.

V

Then, straught or crooked, yird or nane,
　　They roar an' cry a' throw'ther;
The vera *wee-things*, toddlan, rin,
　　Wi' stocks out owre their shouther:
An' gif the *custock's* sweet or sour,
　　Wi' joctelegs they taste them;
Syne coziely, aboon the door,
　　Wi' cannie care, they've plac'd them
　　　　To lye that night.

VI

The lasses staw frae 'mang them a',
　　To pou their *stalks o' corn;*＊
But *Rab* flips out, an' jinks about,
　　Behint the muckle thorn:
He grippet *Nelly*, hard an' fast;
　　Loud skirl'd a' the lasses;
But her *tap-pickle* maist was lost,
　　When kiutlan in the *Fause-house*†
　　　　Wi' him that night.

＊ They go to the barn-yard, and pull each, at three several times, a stalk of Oats. If the third stalk wants the *top pickle*, that is, the grain at the top of the stalk, the party in question will want the Maidenhead.

† When the corn is in a doubtful state, by being too green, or wet, the Stack-builder, by means of old timber, &c. makes a large apartment in his stack, with an opening in the side which is fairest exposed to the wind: this he calls a *Fause-house*.

VII

The auld Guidwife's weel-hoordet *nits**
   Are round an' round divided,
An' monie lads an' lasses fates
   Are there that night decided:
Some kindle, couthie, side by side,
   An' *burn* thegither trimly;
Some start awa, wi' saucy pride,
   An' jump out owre the chimlie
         Fu' high that night.

VIII

Jean slips in twa, wi' tentie e'e;
   Wha 'twas, she wadna tell;
But this is *Jock*, an' this is *me*,
   She says in to hersel:
He bleez'd owre her, an' she owre him,
   As they wad never mair part,
Till fuff! he started up the lum,
   An' *Jean* had e'en a sair heart
         To see't that night.

IX

Poor Willie, wi' his *bow-kail runt*,
   Was *brunt* wi' primsie *Mallie*;
An' *Mary*, nae doubt, took the drunt,
   To be compar'd to *Willie*:
Mall's nit lap out, wi' pridefu' fling,
   An' her ain fit, it brunt it;

---

* Burning the nuts is a favourite charm. They name the lad and lass to each particular nut, as they lay them in the fire; and according as they burn quietly together, or start from beside one another, the course and issue of the Courtship will be.

While *Willie* lap, an' swoor by *jing*,
　　'Twas just the way he wanted
　　　　To be that night.

X

Nell had the *Fause-house* in her min',
　　She pits hersel an' *Rob* in;
In loving bleeze they sweetly join,
　　Till white in ase they're sobbin:
Nell's heart was dancin at the view;
　　She whisper'd *Rob* to leuk for't:
Rob, stownlins, prie'd her bonie mou,
　　Fu' cozie in the neuk for't,
　　　　　Unseen that night.

XI

But *Merran* sat behint their backs,
　　Her thoughts on *Andrew Bell*;
She lea'es them gashan at their cracks,
　　An' slips out by hersel:
She thro' the yard the nearest taks,
　　An' for the *kiln* she goes then,
An' darklins grapet for the *bauks*,
　　And in the *blue-clue** throws then,
　　　　　Right fear't that night.

---

* Whoever would, with success, try this spell, must strictly observe these directions. Steal out, all alone, to the *kiln*, and, darkling, throw into the *pot*, a clew of blue yarn: wind it in a new clew off the old one; and towards the latter end, something will hold the thread: demand, *wha hauds?* i.e. who holds? and answer will be returned from the kiln-pot, by naming the christian and sirname of your future Spouse.

XII

An' ay she *win't,* an' ay she swat,
    I wat she made nae jaukin;
Till something *held* within the *pat,*
    Guid L—d! but she was quaukin!
But whether 'twas the *Deil* himsel,
    Or whether 'twas a *bauk-en',*
Or whether it was *Andrew Bell,*
    She did na wait on talkin
        To spier that night.

XIII

Wee *Jenny* to her Graunie says,
    'Will ye go wi' me Graunie?
I'll *eat the apple** at the *glass,*
    I gat frae uncle Johnie:'
She fuff't her pipe wi' sic a lunt,
    In wrath she was sae vap'rin,
She notic't na, an aizle brunt
    Her braw, new, worset apron
        Out thro' that night.

XIV

'Ye little Skelpie-limmer's-face!
    I daur you try sic sportin,
As seek the *foul Thief* onie place,
    For him to spae your fortune:
Nae doubt but ye may get a *sight!*
    Great cause ye hae to fear it;

---

* Take a candle, and go, alone, to a looking glass: eat an apple before it, and some traditions say you should comb your hair all the time: the face of your conjugal companion, *to be,* will be seen in the glass, as if peeping over your shoulder.

For monie a ane has gotten a fright,
　　An' liv'd an' di'd deleeret,
　　　　On sic a night.

XV

Ae Hairst afore the *Sherra-moor*,
　　I mind't as weel's yestreen,
I was a gilpey then, I'm sure,
　　I was na past fyfteen:
The Simmer had been cauld an' wat,
　　An' *Stuff* was unco green;
An' ay a rantan *Kirn* we gat,
　　An' just on *Halloween*
　　　　It fell that night.

XVI

Our *Stibble-rig* was *Rab McGraen*,
　　A clever, sturdy fallow;
His Sin gat *Eppie Sim* wi' wean,
　　That liv'd in Achmacalla:
He gat *hemp-seed*,* I mind it weel,
　　An' he made unco light o't;
But monie a day was *by himsel*,
　　He was sae fairly frighted
　　　　That vera night.'

* Steal out, unperceived, and sow a handful of hemp seed; harrowing it with any thing you can conveniently draw after you. Repeat, now and then, 'Hemp seed I saw thee, Hemp seed I saw thee; and him (or her) that is to be my true-love, come after me and pou thee.' Look over your left shoulder, and you will see the appearance of the person invoked, in the attitude of pulling hemp. Some traditions say, 'come after me and shaw thee,' that is, show thyself; in which case it simply appears. Others omit the harrowing, and say, 'come after me and harrow thee.'

XVII

Then up gat fechtan *Jamie Fleck*,
    An' he swoor by his conscience,
That he could *saw hemp-seed* a peck;
    For it was a' but nonsense:
The auld guidman raught down the pock,
    An' out a handfu' gied him;
Syne bad him slip frae 'mang the folk,
    Sometime when nae ane see'd him,
                An' try't that night.

XVIII

He marches thro' amang the stacks,
    Tho' he was something sturtan;
The *graip* he for a *harrow* taks,
    An' haurls at his curpan:
And ev'ry now an' then, he says,
    'Hemp-seed I saw thee,
An' her that is to be my lass,
    Come after me an' draw thee
                As fast this night.'

XIX

He whistl'd up *lord Lenox' march*,
    To keep his courage cheary;
Altho' his hair began to arch,
    He was sae fley'd an' eerie:
Till presently he hears a squeak,
    An' then a grane an' gruntle;
He by his showther gae a keek,
    An' tumbl'd wi' a wintle
                Out owre that night.

XX

He roar'd a horrid murder-shout,
　　In dreadfu' desperation!
An' young an' auld come rinnan out,
　　An' hear the sad narration:
He swoor 'twas hilchan *Jean McCraw*,
　　Or crouchie *Merran Humphie*,
Till stop! she trotted thro' them a';
　　An' wha was it but *Grumphie*
　　　　Asteer that night?

XXI

Meg fain wad to the *Barn* gaen,
　　To *winn three wechts o' naething*;*
But for to meet the Deil her lane,
　　She pat but little faith in:
She gies the Herd a pickle nits,
　　An' twa red cheeket apples,
To watch, while for the *Barn* she sets,
　　In hopes to see *Tom Kipples*
　　　　That vera night.

* This charm must likewise be performed, unperceived and alone. You go to the *barn*, and open both doors; taking them off the hinges, if possible; for there is danger, that the Being, about to appear, may shut the doors, and do you some mischief. Then take that instrument used in winnowing the corn, which, in our country-dialect, we call a *wecht*; and go thro' all the attitudes of letting down corn against the wind. Repeat it three times; and the third time, an apparition will pass thro' the barn, in at the windy door, and out at the other, having both the figure in question and the appearance or retinue, marking the employment or station in life.

XXII

She turns the key, wi' cannie thraw,
    An' owre the threshold ventures;
But first on *Sawnie* gies a ca',
    Syne bauldly in she enters:
A *ratton* rattl'd up the wa',
    An' she cry'd, L—d preserve her!
An' ran thro' midden-hole an' a',
    An' pray'd wi' zeal and fervour,
            Fu' fast that night.

XXIII

They hoy't out Will, wi fair advice;
    They hecht him some fine braw ane;
It chanc'd the *Stack* he *faddom't thrice,**
    Was timmer-propt for thrawin:
He taks a swirlie, auld *moss-oak*,
    For some black, grousome *Carlin*;
An' loot a winze, an' drew a stroke,
    Till skin in blypes cam haurlin
            Aff's nieves that night.

XXIV

A wanton widow *Leezie* was,
    As cantie as a kittlen;
But Och! that night, amang the shaws,
    She gat a fearfu' settlin!
She thro' the whins, an' by the cairn,
    An' owre the hill gaed scrievin,

---

* Take an opportunity of going, unnoticed, to a *Bear-stack*, and fathom it three times round. The last fathom of the last time, you will catch in your arms, the appearance of your future conjugal yoke-fellow.

Whare *three Lairds' lan's met at a burn,**
　　To dip her *left sark-sleeve* in,
　　　　Was bent that night.

XXV

Whyles owre a linn the burnie plays,
　　As thro' the glen it wimpl't;
Whyles round a rocky sear it strays;
　　Whyles in a wiel it dimpl't;
Whyles glitter'd to the nightly rays,
　　Wi' bickerin, dancin dazzle;
Whyles cooket underneath the braes,
　　Below the spreading hazle
　　　　Unseen that night.

XXVI

Amang the brachens, on the brae,
　　Between her an' the moon,
The Deil, or else an outler Quey,
　　Gat up an' gae a croon:
Poor *Leezie's* heart maist lap the hool;
　　Near lav'rock-height she jumpet,
But mist a fit, an' in the *pool,*
　　Out owre the lugs she plumpet,
　　　　Wi' a plunge that night.

---

* You go out, one or more, for this is a social spell, to a south-running spring
or rivulet, where 'three Lairds' lands meet', and dip your left shirt sleeve. Go
to bed in sight of a fire, and hang your wet sleeve before it to dry. Ly awake;
and sometime near midnight, an apparition, having the exact figure of the
grand object in question, will come and turn the sleeve, as if to dry the other
side of it.

XXVII

In order, on the clean hearth-stane,
    The *Luggies** three are ranged;
And ev'ry time great care is taen,
    To see them duely changed:
Auld, uncle *John*, wha *wedlock's joys*,
    Sin' *Mar's-year* did desire,
Because he gat the toom dish thrice,
    He heav'd them on the fire,
          In wrath that night.

XXVIII

Wi' merry sangs, an' friendly cracks,
    I wat they did na weary;
And unco tales, an' funnie jokes,
    Their sports were cheap an' cheary:
Till *butter'd So'ns*,† wi' fragrant lunt,
    Set a' their gabs a steerin;
Syne, wi' a social glass o' strunt,
    They parted off careerin
          Fu' blythe that night.

* Take three dishes; put clean water in one, foul water in another, and leave the third empty: blindfold a person, and lead him to the hearth where the dishes are ranged; he (or she) dips the left hand: if by chance in the clean water, the future husband or wife will come to the bar of Matrimony, a Maid; if in the foul, a widow; if in the empty dish, it foretells, with equal certainty, no marriage at all. It is repeated three times; and every time the arrangement of the dishes is altered.

† Sowens, with butter instead of milk to them, is always the *Halloween Supper*.

The auld Farmer's new-year-morning Salutation to his auld Mare, Maggie, on giving her the accustomed ripp of Corn to hansel in the new-year

A *Guid New-year* I wish you Maggie!
Hae, there's a ripp to thy auld baggie:
Tho' thou's howe-backet, now, an' knaggie,
   I've seen the day,
Thou could hae gaen like ony staggie
   Out owre the lay.

 Tho now thou's dowie, stiff an' crazy,
An' thy auld hide as white's a daisie,
I've seen thee dappl't, sleek an' glaizie,
   A bonie gray:
He should been tight that daur't to *raize* thee,
   Ance in a day.

 Thou ance was i' the foremost rank,
A *filly* buirdly, steeve an' swank,
An' set weel down a shapely shank,
   As e'er tread yird;
An' could hae flown out owre a stank,
   Like onie bird.

 It's now some nine-an'-twenty-year,
Sin' thou was my *Guidfather's Meere*;
He gied me thee, o' tocher clear,
   An' fifty mark;
Tho' it was sma', 'twas *weel-won* gear,
   An' thou was stark.

When first I gaed to woo my *Jenny*,
Ye then was trottan wi' your Minnie:
Tho' ye was trickie, flee an' funnie,
            Ye ne'er was donsie;
But hamely, tawie, quiet an' cannie,
            An' unco sonsie.

That *day*, ye pranc'd wi' muckle pride,
When ye bure hame my bonie *Bride*:
An' sweet an' gracefu' she did ride
            Wi' maiden air!
Kyle-Stewart I could bragged wide,
            For sic a *pair*.

Tho' now ye dow but hoyte and hoble,
An' wintle like a saumont coble,
That day, ye was a jinker noble,
            For heels an' win'!
An' ran them till they a' did wauble,
            Far, far behin'!

When thou an' I were young an' skiegh,
An' *Stable-meals* at Fairs were driegh,
How thou wad prance, an' snore, an' scriegh,
            An' tak the road!
Towns-bodies ran, an' stood abiegh,
            An' ca't thee mad.

When thou was corn't, an' I was mellow,
We took the road ay like a Swallow:
At *Brooses* thou had ne'er a fellow,
            For pith an' speed;
But ev'ry tail thou pay't them hollow,
            Whare'er thou gaed.

The sma', droot-rumpl't, hunter cattle,
Might aiblins, waur't thee for a brattle;
But *sax Scotch mile*, thou try't their mettle,
      An' gart them whaizle:
Nae whip nor spur, but just a wattle
      O' saugh or hazle.

Thou was a noble *Fittie-lan'*,
As e'er in tug or tow was drawn!
Aft thee an' I, in aught hours gaun,
      On guid March-weather,
Hae turn'd *sax rood* beside our han',
      For days thegither.

Thou never braing't, an' fetch't, an' flisket,
But thy *auld tail* thou wad hae whisket,
An' spread abreed thy weel-fill'd *brisket*,
      Wi' pith an' pow'r,
Till sprittie knowes wad rair't an' risket,
      An' slypet owre.

When frosts lay lang, an' snaws were deep,
An' threaten'd *labor* back to keep,
I gied thy *cog* a wee-bit heap
      Aboon the timmer;
I ken'd my *Maggie* wad na sleep
      For that, or Simmer.

In *cart* or *car* thou never reestet;
The steyest brae thou wad hae fac't it;
Thou never lap, an' sten't, an' breastet,
      Then stood to blaw;
But just thy step a wee thing hastet,
      Thou snoov't awa.

My Pleugh is now thy *bairn-time* a';
Four gallant brutes, as e'er did draw;
Forby sax mae, I've sell't awa,
   That thou hast nurst:
They drew me thretteen pund an' twa,
   The vera warst.

Monie a sair daurk we twa hae wrought,
An' wi' the weary warl' fought!
An' monie an' *anxious day*, I thought
   We wad be beat!
Yet here to *crazy Age* we're brought,
   Wi' something yet.

An' think na, my auld, trusty *Servan'*,
That now perhaps thou's less deservin,
An' thy *auld days* may end in starvin',
   For my last fow,
A heapet *Stimpart*, I'll reserve ane
   Laid by for you.

We've worn to crazy years thegither;
We'll toyte about wi' ane anither;
Wi' tentie care I'll flit thy tether,
   To some hain'd rig,
Whare ye may nobly rax your leather,
   Wi' sma' fatigue.

The Cotter's Saturday Night

INSCRIBED TO R. A**** ESQ

Let not Ambition mock their useful toil,
Their homely joys, and destiny obscure;
Nor Grandeur hear, with a disdainful smile,
The short and simple annals of the Poor.

GRAY

I

My lov'd, my honor'd, much respected friend,
  No mercenary Bard his homage pays;
With honest pride, I scorn each selfish end,
  My dearest meed, a friend's esteem and praise:
To you I sing, in simple Scottish lays,
  The *lowly train* in life's sequester'd scene;
The native feelings strong, the guileless ways,
  What A**** in a *Cottage* would have been;
Ah! tho' his worth unknown, far happier there I ween!

II

November chill blaws loud wi' angry sugh;
  The short'ning winter-day is near a close;
The miry beasts retreating frae the pleugh;
  The black'ning trains o' craws to their repose:
The toil-worn Cotter frae his labor goes,
  This night his weekly moil is at an end,
Collects his *spades*, his *mattocks* and his *hoes*,
  Hoping the *morn* in ease and rest to spend,
And weary, o'er the moor, his course does hameward bend.

III

At length his lonely *Cot* appears in view,
 Beneath the shelter of an aged tree;
The expectant *wee-things*, toddlan, stacher through
 To meet their *Dad*, wi' flichterin noise and glee.
His wee-bit ingle, blinkan bonilie,
 His clean hearth-stane, his thrifty *Wifie's* smile,
The *lisping infant*, prattling on his knee,
 Does a' his weary *kiaugh* and care beguile,
And makes him quite forget his labor and his toil.

VI

Belyve, the *elder bairns* come drapping in,
 At *Service* out, amang the Farmers roun';
Some ca' the pleugh, some herd, some tentie rin
 A cannie errand to a neebor town:
Their eldest hope, their *Jenny*, woman-grown,
 In youthfu' bloom, Love sparkling in her e'e,
Comes hame, perhaps, to shew a braw new gown,
 Or deposite her fair-won penny-fee,
To help her *Parents* dear, if they in hardship be.

V

With joy unfeign'd, *brothers* and *sisters* meet,
 And each for other's weelfare kindly spiers:
The social hours, swift-wing'd, unnotic'd fleet;
 Each tells the uncos that he sees or hears.
The Parents partial eye their hopeful years;
 Anticipation forward points the view;
The *Mother*, wi' her needle and her sheers,
 Gars auld claes look amaist as weel's the new;
The *Father* mixes a' wi' admonition due.

VI

Their Master's and their Mistress's command,
    The *youngkers* a' are warned to obey;
And mind their labors wi' an eydent hand,
    And ne'er, tho' out o' sight, to jauk or play:
'And O! be sure to fear the Lord alway!
    And mind your *duty*, duely, morn and night!
Lest in temptation's path ye gang astray,
    Implore his *counsel* and assisting *might*:
They never sought in vain that sought the Lord aright.'

VII

But hark! a rap comes gently to the door;
    Jenny, wha kens the meaning o' the same,
Tells how a neebor lad came o'er the moor,
    To do some errands, and convoy her hame.
The wily Mother sees the *conscious flame*
    Sparkle in *Jenny's* e'e, and flush her cheek,
With heart-struck, anxious care enquires his name,
    While *Jenny* hafflins is afraid to speak;
Weel-pleas'd the Mother hears, it's nae wild, worthless *Rake*.

VIII

With kindly welcome, *Jenny* brings him ben;
    A *strappan youth*; he takes the Mother's eye;
Blythe *Jenny* sees the *visit's* no ill taen;
    The Father cracks of horses, pleughs and kye.
The *Youngster's* artless heart o'erflows wi' joy,
    But blate and laithfu', scarce can weel behave;
The Mother, wi' a woman's wiles, can spy
    What makes the *youth* sae bashfu' and sae grave;
Weel-pleas'd to think her *bairn's* respected like the lave.

IX

O happy love! where love like this is found!
  O heart-felt raptures! bliss beyond compare!
I've paced much this weary, *mortal round*,
  And sage Experience bids me this declare –
'If Heaven a draught of heavenly pleasure spare,
  One *cordial* in this melancholy *Vale*,
'Tis when a youthful, loving, *modest* Pair,
  In other's arms, breathe out the tender tale,
Beneath the milk-white thorn that scents the ev'ning gale.'

X

Is there, in human form, that bears a heart –
  A Wretch! a Villain! lost to love and truth!
That can, with studied, sly, ensnaring art,
  Betray sweet Jenny's unsuspecting youth?
Curse on his perjur'd arts! dissembling smooth!
  Are *Honor, Virtue, Conscience*, all exil'd?
Is there no Pity, no relenting Ruth,
  Points to the Parents fondling o'er their Child?
Then paints the *ruin'd Maid*, and *their* distraction wild!

XI

But now the Supper crowns their simple board,
  The healsome *Porritch*, chief of Scotia's food:
The soupe their *only Hawkie* does afford,
  That 'yont the hallan snugly chows her cood:
The *Dame* brings forth, in complimental mood,
  To grace the lad, her weel-hain'd kebbuck, fell,
And aft he's prest, and aft he ca's it guid;
  The frugal *Wifie*, garrulous, will tell.
How 'twas a towmond auld, sin' Lint was i' the bell.

XII

The chearfu' Supper done, wi' serious face,
    They, round the ingle, form a circle wide;
The Sire turns o'er, with patriarchal grace,
    The big *ha'-Bible*, ance his *Father's* pride:
His bonnet rev'rently is laid aside,
    His *lyart haffets* wearing thin and bare;
Those strains that once did sweet in Zion glide,
    He wales a portion with judicious care;
'*And let us worship God!*' he says with solemn air.

XIII

They chant their artless notes in simple guise;
    They tune their *hearts*, by far the noblest aim:
Perhaps *Dundee's* wild warbling measures rise,
    Or plaintive *Martyrs*, worthy of the name;
Or noble *Elgin* beets the heaven-ward flame,
    The sweetest far of Scotia's holy lays;
Compar'd with these, *Italian trills* are tame;
    The tickl'd ears no heart-felt raptures raise;
Nae unison hae they, with our Creator's praise.

XIV

The priest-like Father reads the sacred page,
    How *Abram* was the Friend of God on high;
Or, *Moses* bade eternal warfare wage,
    With *Amalek's* ungracious progeny;
Or how the *royal Bard* did groaning lye,
    Beneath the stroke of Heaven's avenging ire;
Or *Job's* pathetic plaint, and wailing cry;
    Or rapt *Isaiah's* wild, seraphic fire;
Or other *Holy Seers* that tune the *sacred lyre*.

XV

Perhaps the *Christian Volume* is the theme,
  How *guiltless blood* for *guilty man* was shed;
How He, who bore in heaven the second name,
  Had not on Earth whereon to lay His head:
How His first *followers* and *servants* sped;
  The *Precepts sage* they wrote to many a land:
How *he*, who lone in *Patmos* banished,
  Saw in the sun a mighty angel stand;
And heard great *Bab'lon's* doom pronounc'd by Heaven's
    command.

XVI

Then kneeling down to Heaven's Eternal King,
  The *Saint*, the *Father*, and the *Husband* prays:
Hope 'springs exulting on triumphant wing,'*
  That *thus* they all shall meet in future days:
There, ever bask in *uncreated rays*,
  No more to sigh, or shed the bitter tear,
Together hymning their Creator's praise,
  In *such society*, yet still more dear;
While circling Time moves round in an eternal sphere.

XVII

Compar'd with *this*, how poor Religion's pride,
  In all the pomp of *method*, and of *art*,
When men display to congregations wide,
  Devotion's ev'ry grace, except the *heart!*
The Power, incens'd, the Pageant will desert,
  The pompous strain, the sacredotal stole;
But haply, in some *Cottage* far apart,
  May hear, well pleas'd, the language of the *Soul*;
And in His *Book of Life* the Inmates poor enroll.

* Pope's *Windsor Forest.*

XVIII

Then homeward all take off their sev'ral way;
  The youngling *Cottagers* retire to rest:
The Parent-pair their *secret homage* pay,
  And proffer up to Heaven the warm request,
That He who stills the *raven's* clam'rous nest,
  And decks the *lily* fair in flow'ry pride,
Would, in the way *His Wisdom* sees the best,
  For *them* and for their *little ones* provide;
But chiefly, in their hearts with *Grace divine* preside.

XIX

From scenes like these, old Scotia's grandeur springs,
  That makes her lov'd at home, rever'd abroad:
Princes and lords are but the breath of kings,
  'An honest man's the noble work of God:'
And *certes*, in fair Virtue's heavenly road,
  The *Cottage* leaves the *Palace* far behind:
What is a lordling's pomp? a cumbrous load,
  Disguising oft the *wretch* of human kind,
Studied in arts of Hell, in wickedness refin'd!

XX

O Scotia! my dear, my native soil!
  For whom my warmest wish to heaven is sent!
Long may thy hardy sons of *rustic toil*,
  Be blest with health, and peace, and sweet content!
And O may Heaven their simple lives prevent
  From *Luxury's* contagion, weak and vile!
Then howe'er *crowns* and *coronets* be rent,
  A *virtuous Populace* may rise the while,
And stand a wall of fire around their much-lov'd Isle.

XXI

O Thou! who pour'd the *patriotic tide*,
　　That stream'd thro' great, unhappy Wallace' heart;
Who dar'd to, nobly, stem tyrannic pride,
　　Or *nobly die*, the second glorious part:
(The Patriot's God, peculiarly thou art,
　　His *friend, inspirer, guardian* and *reward!*)
O never, never Scotia's realm desert,
　　But still the *Patriot*, and the *Patriot-Bard*,
In bright succession raise, her *Ornament* and *Guard!*

To a Mouse,

On turning her up in her Nest, with the Plough,
November 1785

Wee, sleeket, cowran, tim'rous *beastie*,
O, what a panic's in thy breastie!
Thou need na start awa sae hasty,
      Wi' bickering brattle!
I wad be laith to rin an' chase thee,
      Wi' murd'ring *pattle!*

I'm truly sorry Man's dominion
Has broken Nature's social union,
An' justifies that ill opinion,
      Which makes thee startle,
At me, thy poor, earth-born companion,
      An' *fellow-mortal!*

I doubt na, whyles, but thou may *thieve*;
What then? poor beastie, thou maun live!
A *daimen-icker* in a *thrave*
      'S a sma' request:
I'll get a blessin wi' the lave,
      An' never miss't!

Thy wee-bit *housie*, too, in ruin!
It's silly wa's the win's are strewin!
An' naething, now, to big a new ane,
      O' foggage green!
An' bleak *December's winds* ensuin,
      Baith snell an' keen!

Thou saw the fields laid bare an' wast,
An' weary *Winter* comin fast,
An' cozie here, beneath the blast,
      Thou thought to dwell,
Till crash! the cruel *coulter* past
      Out thro' thy cell.

That wee-bit heap o' leaves an stibble,
Has cost thee monie a weary nibble!
Now thou's turn'd out, for a' thy trouble,
      But house or hald,
To thole the Winter's *sleety dribble,*
      An' *cranreuch* cauld!

But Mousie, thou art no thy-lane,
In proving *foresight* may be vain:
The best laid schemes o' *Mice* an' *Men,*
      Gang aft agley,
An' lea'e us nought but grief an' pain,
      For promis'd joy!

Still, thou art blest, compar'd wi' *me!*
The *present* only toucheth thee:
But Och! I *backward* cast my e'e,
      On prospects drear!
An' *forward,* tho' I canna *see,*
      I *guess* an' *fear!*

Epistle to Davie, a brother Poet

January————

I

While winds frae off Ben-Lomond blaw,
And bar the doors wi' driving snaw,
　　And hing us owre the ingle,
I set me down, to pass the time,
And spin a verse or twa o' rhyme,
　　In hamely, *westlin* jingle.
While frosty winds blaw in the drift,
　　Ben to the chimla lug,
I grudge a wee the *Great-folk's* gift,
　　That live sae bien an' snug:
　　　　I tent less, and want less
　　　　　　Their roomy fire-side;
　　　　But hanker, and canker,
　　　　　　To see their cursed pride.

II

It's hardly in a body's pow'r,
To keep, at times, frae being sour,
　　To see how things are shar'd;
How *best o' chiels* are whyles in want,
While *Cooss* on countless thousands rant,
　　And ken na how to wair't:
But Davie lad, ne'er fash your head,
　　Tho' we hae little gear,
We're fit to win our daily bread,
　　As lang's we're hale and fier:
　　　　'Mair spier na, nor fear na,'*

* Ramsay.

Auld age ne'er mind a seg;
The last o't, the warst o't,
 Is only but to beg.

III

To lye in kilns and barns at e'en,
When banes are craz'd, and bluid is thin,
 Is, doubtless, great distress!
Yet then *content* could make us blest;
Ev'n then, sometimes we'd snatch a taste
 Of truest happiness.
The honest heart that's free frae a'
 Intended fraud or guile,
However Fortune kick the ba',
 Has ay some cause to smile:
  And mind still, you'll find still,
   A comfort this nae sma';
  Nae mair then, we'll care then
   Nae *farther* we can *fa'*.

IV

What tho', like Commoners of air,
We wander out, we know not where,
 But either house or hal'?
Yet *Nature's* charms, the hills and woods,
The sweeping vales, and foaming floods,
 Are free alike to all.
In days when Daisies deck the ground,
 And Blackbirds whistle clear,
With honest joy, our hearts will bound,
 To see the *coming* year:
  On braes when we please then,
   We'll sit and *sowth* a tune;
  Syne *rhyme* till't, well time till't,
   And sing't when we hae done.

V

It's no in titles nor in rank;
It's no in wealth like *Lon'on Bank*,
  To purchase peace and rest;
It's no in makin muckle, *mair*:
It's no in books; it's no in Lear,
  To make us truly blest:
If Happiness hae not her seat
  And center in the breast,
We may be *wise*, or *rich*, or *great*,
  But never can be *blest*:
    Nae treasures, nor pleasures
      Could make us happy lang;
    The *heart* ay's the part ay,
      That makes us right or wrang.

VI

Think ye, that sic as *you* and *I*,
Wha drudge and drive thro' wet and dry,
  Wi' never-ceasing toil;
Think ye, are we less blest than they,
Wha scarcely tent us in their way,
  As hardly worth their while?
Alas! how aft, in haughty mood,
  God's creatures they oppress!
Or else, neglecting a' that's guid,
  They riot in excess!
    Baith careless, and fearless,
      Of either Heaven or Hell;
    Esteeming, and deeming,
      It a' an idle tale!

VII

Then let us chearful' acquiesce;
Nor make our scanty Pleasures less,
 By pining at our state:
And, ev'n should Misfortunes come,
I, here wha sit, hae met wi' some,
 An's thankfu' for them yet.
They gie the wit of *Age* to *Youth*;
 They let us ken oursel;
They make us see the naked truth.
 The *real* guid and ill.
  Tho' losses, and crosses,
   Be lessons right severe,
  There's *wit* there, ye'll get there,
   Ye'll find nae other wherc.

VIII

But tent me, Davie, *Ace o' Hearts!*
(To say aught less wad wrang the *cartes*,
 And flatt'ry I detest)
This life has joys for you and I;
And joys that riches ne'er could buy;
 And joys the very best.
There's a' the *Pleasures o' the Heart*,
 The *Lover* and the *Frien'*;
Ye hae your Meg, your dearest part.
 And I my darling Jean!
  It warms me, it charms me,
   To mention but her *name*:
  It heats me, it beets me,
   And sets me a' on flame!

IX

O, all ye *Pow'rs* who rule above!
O Thou, whose very self art *love*!
 Thou know'st my words sincere!
The *life blood* streaming thro' my heart,
Or my more dear *Immortal part*,
 Is not more fondly dear!
When heart-corroding care and grief
 Deprive my soul of rest,
Her dear idea brings relief,
 And solace to my breast.
  Thou Being, Allseeing,
   O hear my fervent pray'r!
  Still take her, and make her,
   Thy most peculiar care!

X

All hail! ye tender feelings dear!
The smile of love, the friendly tear,
 The sympathetic glow!
Long since, this world's thorny ways
Had number'd out my weary days,
 Had it not been for you!
Fate still has blest me with a friend,
 In ev'ry care and ill;
And oft a more *endearing* band,
 A *tye* more tender still.
  It lightens, it brightens,
   The tenebrific scene,
  To meet with, and greet with,
   My Davie or my Jean!

XI

O, how that *name* inspires my style!
The words come skelpan, rank and file,
   Amaist before I ken!
The ready measure rins as fine,
As *Phœbus* and the famous *Nine*
   Were glowran owre my pen.
My spavet *Pegasus* will limp,
   Till ance he's fairly het;
And then he'll hilch, and stilt, and jimp,
   And rin an unco fit:
     But least then, the beast then,
      Should rue this hasty ride,
     I'll light now, and dight now,
      His sweaty, wizen'd hide.

The Lament

OCCASIONED BY THE UNFORTUNATE
ISSUE OF A FRIEND'S AMOUR

Alas! how oft does goodness wound itself?
And sweet Affection *prove the spring of Woe!*

HOME

I

O Thou pale Orb, that silent shines,
   While care-untroubled mortals sleep!
Thou seest a *wretch*, who inly pines,
   And wanders here to wail and weep!
With Woe I nightly vigils keep,
   Beneath thy wan, unwarming beam;
And mourn, in lamentation deep,
   How *life* and *love* are all a dream!

II

I joyless view thy rays adorn,
   The faintly-marked, distant hill:
I joyless view thy trembling horn,
   Reflected in the gurgling rill.
My fondly-fluttering heart, be still!
   Thou busy pow'r, Remembrance, cease!
Ah! must the agonizing thrill,
   For ever bar returning Peace!

III

No idly-feign'd, poetic pains,
   My sad, lovelorn lamentings claim:
No shepherd's pipe – Arcadian strains;
   No fabled tortures, quaint and tame.

The *plighted faith*; the *mutual flame*;
   The *oft-attested Powers above*;
The *promis'd Father's tender name*;
   These were the pledges of my love!

IV

Encircled in her clasping arms,
   How have the raptur'd moments flown!
How have I wish'd for Fortune's charms,
   For her dear sake, and her's alone!
And, must I think it! is she gone,
   My secret-heart's exulting boast?
And does she heedless hear my groan?
   And is she ever, ever lost?

V

Oh! can she bear so base a heart,
   So lost to Honor, lost to Truth,
As from the *fondest lover* part,
   The *plighted husband* of her youth?
Alas! Life's path may be unsmooth!
   Her way may lie thro' rough distress!
Then, who her pangs and pains will soothe,
   Her sorrows share and make them less?

VI

Ye winged Hours that o'er us past,
   Enraptur'd more, the more enjoy'd,
Your dear remembrance in my breast,
   My fondly-treasur'd thoughts employ'd.
That breast, how dreary now, and void,
   For her too scanty once of room!
Ev'n ev'ry *ray* of *Hope* destroy'd,
   And not a *Wish* to gild the gloom!

VII

The morn that warns th'approaching day,
    Awakes me up to toil and woe:
I see the hours, in long array,
    That I must suffer, lingering, slow.
Full many a pang, and many a throe,
    Keen Recollection's direful train,
Must wring my soul, ere Phœbus, low,
    Shall kiss the distant, western main.

VIII

And when my nightly couch I try,
    Sore-harass'd out, with care and grief,
My toil-beat nerves, and tear-worn eye,
    Keep watchings with the nightly thief:
Or if I slumber, Fancy, chief,
    Reigns, hagard-wild, in sore afright:
Ev'n day, all-bitter, brings relief,
    From such a horror-breathing night.

IX

O! thou bright Queen, who, o'er th'expanse,
    Now highest reign'st, with boundless sway!
Oft has thy silent-marking glance
    Observ'd us, fondly-wand'ring, stray!
The time, unheeded, sped away,
    While Love's *luxurious pulse* beat high,
Beneath thy silver-gleaming ray,
    To mark the mutual-kindling eye.

X

Oh! scenes in strong remembrance set!
    Scenes, never, never to return!
Scenes, if in stupor I forget,
    Again I feel, again I burn!

From ev'ry joy and pleasure torn,
  Life's weary vale I'll wander thro';
And hopeless, comfortless, I'll mourn
  A faithless woman's broken vow.

Despondency, an Ode

I

Oppress'd with grief, oppress'd with care,
A burden more than I can bear,
  I set me down and sigh:
O Life! Thou art a galling load,
Along a rough, a weary road,
  To wretches such as I!
Dim-backward as I cast my view,
  What sick'ning Scenes appear!
What Sorrows *yet* may pierce me thro',
  Too justly I may fear!
    Still caring, despairing,
      Must be my bitter doom;
    My woes here, shall close ne'er,
      But with the *closing tomb!*

II

Happy! ye sons of Busy-life,
Who, equal to the bustling strife,
  No other view regard!
Ev'n when the wished *end's* deny'd,
Yet while the busy *means* are ply'd,
  They bring their own reward:
Whilst I, a hope-abandon'd wight,
  Unfitted with an *aim*,
Meet ev'ry sad-returning night,
  And joyless morn the same.
    You, bustling and justling,
      Forget each grief and pain;
    I, listless, yet restless,
      Find ev'ry prospect vain.

III

How blest the Solitary's lot,
Who, all-forgetting, all-forgot,
   Within his humble cell,
The cavern wild with tangling roots,
Sits o'er his newly-gather'd fruits,
   Beside his crystal well!
Or haply, to his ev'ning thought,
   By unfrequented stream,
The *ways of men* are distant brought,
   A faint-collected dream:
     While praising, and raising
      His thoughts to Heaven on high,
     As wand'ring, meand'ring,
      He views the solemn sky.

IV

Than I, no *lonely Hermit* plac'd
Where never human footstep trac'd,
   Less fit to play the part,
The *lucky moment* to improve,
And *just* to stop, and *just* to move,
   With *self-respecting* art:
But ah! those pleasures, Loves and Joys,
   Which I too keenly taste,
The *Solitary* can despise,
   Can want, and yet be blest!
     He needs not, he heeds not,
      Or human love or hate;
     Whilst I here, must cry here,
      At perfidy ingrate!

v

Oh, enviable, early days,
When dancing thoughtless Pleasure's maze,
  To Care, to Guilt unknown!
How ill exchang'd for riper times,
To feel the follies, or the crimes,
  Of others, or my own!
Ye tiny elves that guiltless sport,
  Like linnets in the bush,
Ye little know the ills ye court,
  When Manhood is your wish!
    The losses, the crosses,
      That *active man* engage;
    The fears all, the tears all,
      Of dim declining *Age!*

Man was made to mourn,
a Dirge

I

When chill November's surly blast
   Made fields and forests bare,
One ev'ning, as I wand'red forth,
   Along the banks of Aire,
I spy'd a man, whose aged step
   Seem'd weary, worn with care;
His face was furrow'd o'er with years,
   And hoary was his hair.

II

Young stranger, whither wand'rest thou?
   Began the rev'rend Sage;
Does thirst of wealth thy step constrain,
   Or youthful Pleasure's rage?
Or haply, prest with cares and woes,
   Too soon thou hast began,
To wander forth, with me, to mourn
   The miseries of Man.

III

The Sun that overhangs yon moors,
   Out-spreading far and wide,
Where hundreds labour to support
   A haughty lordling's pride;
I've seen yon weary winter-sun
   Twice forty times return;
And ev'ry time has added proofs,
   That Man was made to mourn.

IV

O Man! while in thy early years,
How prodigal of time!
Mispending all thy precious hours,
Thy glorious, youthful prime!
Alternate Follies take the sway;
Licentious Passions burn;
Which tenfold force gives Nature's law,
That Man was made to mourn.

V

Look not alone on youthful Prime,
Or Manhood's active might;
Man then is useful to his kind,
Supported is his right:
But see him on the edge of life,
With Cares and Sorrows worn,
Then Age and Want, Oh! ill-match'd pair!
Show Man was made to mourn.

VI

A few seem favourites of Fate,
In Pleasure's lap carest;
Yet, think not all the Rich and Great,
Are likewise truly blest.
But Oh! what crouds in ev'ry land,
All wretched and forlorn,
Thro' weary life this lesson learn,
That Man was made to mourn!

VII

Many and sharp the num'rous Ills
Inwoven with our frame!
More pointed still we make ourselves,
Regret, Remorse and Shame!

And Man, whose heav'n-erected face,
   The smiles of love adorn,
Man's inhumanity to Man
   Makes countless thousands mourn!

VIII

See, yonder poor, o'erlabour'd wight,
   So abject, mean and vile,
Who begs a brother of the earth
   To give him leave to toil;
And see his lordly *fellow-worm*,
   The poor petition spurn,
Unmindful, tho' a weeping wife,
   And helpless offspring mourn.

IX

If I'm design'd yon lordling's slave,
   By Nature's law design'd,
Why was an independent wish
   E'er planted in my mind?
If not, why am I subject to
   His cruelty, or scorn?
Or why has Man the will and pow'r
   To make his fellow mourn?

X

Yet, let not this too much, my Son,
   Disturb thy youthful breast:
This partial view of human-kind
   Is surely not the *last!*
The poor, oppressed, honest man
   Had never, sure, been born,
Had there not been some recompence
   To comfort those that mourn!

XI

O Death! the poor man's dearest friend,
    The kindest and the best!
Welcome the hour, my aged limbs
    Are laid with thee at rest!
The Great, the Wealthy fear thy blow,
    From pomp and pleasure torn;
But Oh! a blest relief for those
    That weary-laden mourn!

Winter, a Dirge

I

The Wintry West extends his blast,
    And hail and rain does blaw;
Or, the stormy North sends driving forth,
    The blinding sleet and snaw:
While, tumbling brown, the Burn comes down,
    And roars frae bank to brae;
And bird and beast, in covert, rest,
    And pass the heartless day.

II

'The sweeping blast, the sky o'ercast,'*
    The joyless *winter-day*,
Let others fear, to me more dear,
    Than all the pride of May:
The Tempest's howl, it *soothes* my soul,
    My *griefs* it seems to join;
The leafless trees my fancy please,
    Their *fate* resembles mine!

III

Thou Pow'r Supreme, whose mighty Scheme,
    These *woes* of mine fulfil;
Here, firm, I rest, they *must* be best,
    Because they are *Thy* Will!
Then all I want (Oh, do thou grant
    This one request of mine!)
Since to *enjoy* Thou dost deny,
    Assist me to *resign!*

* Dr Young.

A Prayer
in the prospect of Death

I

O Thou unknown, Almighty Cause
  Of all my hope and fear!
In whose dread Presence, ere an hour,
  Perhaps I must appear!

II

If I have wander'd in those paths
  Of life I ought to shun;
As *Something*, loudly, in my breast,
  Remonstrates I have done;

III

Thou know'st that Thou hast formed me,
  With Passions wild and strong;
And list'ning to their witching voice
  Has often led me wrong.

IV

Where human *weakness* has come short,
  Or *frailty* stept aside,
Do Thou, All-Good, for such Thou art,
  In shades of darkness hide.

V

Where with *intention* I have err'd,
  No other plea I have,
But, *Thou art good*, and Goodness still
  Delighteth to forgive.

To a Mountain-Daisy,

On turning one down, with the Plough, in April 1786

Wee, modest, crimson-tipped flow'r,
Thou's met me in an evil hour;
For I maun crush amang the stoure
  Thy slender stem:
To spare thee now is past my pow'r,
  Thou bonie gem.

Alas! it's no thy neebor sweet,
The bonie *Lark*, companion meet!
Bending thee 'mang the dewy weet!
  Wi's spreckl'd breast,
When upward-springing, blythe, to greet
  The purpling East.

Cauld blew the bitter-biting *North*
Upon thy early, humble birth;
Yet chearfully thou glinted forth
  Amid the storm,
Scarce rear'd above the *Parent-earth*
  Thy tender form.

The flaunting *flow'rs* our Gardens yield,
High-shelt'ring woods and wa's maun shield,
But thou, beneath the random bield
  O' clod or stane,
Adorns the histie *stibble-field*,
  Unseen, alane.

There, in thy scanty mantle clad,
Thy snawie bosom sun-ward spread,
Thou lifts thy unassuming head
       In humble guise;
But now the *share* uptears thy bed,
       And low thou lies!

Such is the fate of artless Maid,
Sweet *flow'ret* of the rural shade!
By Love's simplicity betray'd,
       And guileless trust,
Till she, like thee, all soil'd, is laid
       Low i' the dust.

Such is the fate of simple Bard,
On Life's rough ocean luckless starr'd!
Unskilful he to note the card
       Of *prudent Lore*,
Till billows rage, and gales blow hard,
       And whelm him o'er!

Such fate to *suffering worth* is giv'n,
Who long with wants and woes has striv'n,
By human pride or cunning driv'n
       To Mis'ry's brink,
Till wrench'd of ev'ry stay but Heav'n,
       He, ruin'd, sink!

Ev'n thou who mourn'st the *Daisy's* fate,
That fate is thine – no distant date;
Stern Ruin's *plough-share* drives, elate,
       Full on thy bloom,
Till crush'd beneath the *furrow's* weight,
       Shall be thy doom!

To Ruin

I

All hail! inexorable lord!
At whose destruction-breathing word,
  The mightiest empires fall!
Thy cruel, woe-delighted train,
The ministers of Grief and Pain,
  A sullen welcome, all!
With stern-resolv'd, despairing eye,
  I see each aimed dart;
For one has cut my *dearest tye*,
  And quivers in my heart.
    Then low'ring, and pouring,
      The *Storm* no more I dread;
    Tho' thick'ning, and black'ning,
      Round my devoted head.

II

And thou grim Pow'r, by Life abhorr'd,
While Life a *pleasure* can afford,
  Oh! hear a wretch's pray'r!
No more I shrink appall'd, afraid;
I court, I beg thy friendly aid,
  To close this scene of care!
When shall my soul, in silent peace,
  Resign Life's *joyless* day?
My weary heart its throbbings cease,
  Cold-mould'ring in the clay?
    No fear more, no tear more,
      To stain my lifeless face,
    Enclasped, and grasped,
      Within thy cold embrace!

Epistle to a young Friend

May – 1786

I

I Lang hae thought, my youthfu' friend,
    A Something to have sent you,
Tho' it should serve nae other end
    Than just a kind memento;
But how the subject theme may gang,
    Let time and chance determine;
Perhaps it may turn out a Sang;
    Perhaps, turn out a Sermon.

II

Ye'll try the world soon my lad,
    And Andrew dear believe me,
Ye'll find mankind an unco squad,
    And muckle they may grieve ye:
For care and trouble set your thought,
    Ev'n when your end's attained;
And a' your views may come to nought
    Where ev'ry nerve is strained.

III

I'll no say, men are villains a';
    The real, harden'd wicked,
Wha hae nae check but *human law*,
    Are to a few restricked:
But Och, mankind are unco weak,
    An' little to be trusted;
If *Self* the wavering balance shake,
    It's rarely right adjusted!

IV

Yet they wha fa' in Fortune's strife,
    Their fate we should na censure,
For still th' *important end* of life,
    They equally may answer:
A man may hae an *honest heart*,
    Tho' Poortith hourly stare him;
A man may tak a neebor's part,
    Yet hae nae *cash* to spare him.

V

Ay free, aff han', your story tell,
    When wi' a bosom crony;
But still keep something to yoursel
    Ye scarcely tell to ony.
Conceal yoursel as weel's yc can
    Frae critical dissection;
But keek thro' ev'ry other man,
    Wi' sharpen'd, sly inspection.

VI

The *sacred lowe* o' weel plac'd love,
    Luxuriantly indulge it;
But never tempt th'*illicit rove*,
    Tho' naething should divulge it:
I wave the quantum o' the sin;
    The hazard of concealing;
But Och! it hardens *a' within*,
    And petrifies the feeling!

VII

To catch Dame Fortune's golden smile,
    Assiduous wait upon her;
And gather gear by ev'ry wile,
    That's justify'd by Honor:

Not for to *hide* it in a *hedge*,
  Nor for a *train-attendant*;
But for the glorious priviledge
  Of being *independant*.

VIII

The *fear o' Hell's* a hangman's whip,
  To haud the wretch in order;
But where ye feel your *Honor* grip,
  Let that ay be your border:
It's slightest touches, instant pause –
  Debar a' side-pretences;
And resolutely keep its laws,
  Uncaring consequences.

IX

The great Creator to revere,
  Must sure become the *Creature*;
But still the preaching cant forbear,
  And ev'n the rigid feature:
Yet ne'er with Wits prophane to range,
  Be complaisance extended;
An *athiest-laugh's* a poor exchange
  For *Deity offended!*

X

When ranting round in Pleasure's ring,
  Religion may be blinded;
Or if she gie a *random-sting*,
  It may be little minded;
But when on Life we're tempest-driven,
  A Conscience but a canker –
A correspondence fix'd wi' Heav'n,
  Is sure a noble *anchor!*

XI

Adieu, dear, amiable Youth!
  Your *heart* can ne'er be wanting!
May Prudence, Fortitude and Truth
  Erect your brow, undaunting!
In *ploughman phrase* 'God send you speed,'
  Still daily to grow wiser;
And may ye better reck the *rede*,
  Than ever did th' *Adviser!*

On a Scotch Bard
gone to the West Indies

A' Ye wha live by sowps o' drink,
A' ye wha live by crambo-clink,
A' ye wha live and never think,
      Come, mourn wi' me!
Our *billie's* gien us a' a jink,
      An' owre the Sea.

Lament him a' ye rantan core,
Wha dearly like a random-splore;
Nae mair he'll join the *merry roar*,
      In social key;
For now he's taen anither shore,
      An' owre the Sea!

The bonie lasses weel may wiss him,
And in their dear *petitions* place him:
The widows, wives, an' a' may bless him,
      Wi' tearfu' e'e;
For weel I wat they'll fairly miss him
      That's owre the Sea!

O Fortune, they hae room to grumble!
Hadst thou taen aff some drowsy bummle,
Wha can do nought but fyke an' fumble,
      'Twad been nae plea;
But he was gleg as onie wumble,
      That's owre the Sea!

Auld, cantie Kyle may weepers wear,
An' stain them wi' the saut, saut tear:
'Twill mak her poor, auld heart, I fear,
    In flinders flee:
He was her *Laureat* monie a year,
      That's owre the Sea!

He saw Misfortune's cauld *Nor-west*
Lang-mustering up a bitter blast;
A Jillet brak his heart at last,
    Ill may she be!
So, took a birth afore the mast,
      An' owre the Sea.

To tremble under Fortune's cummock,
On scarce a bellyfu' o' *drummock*,
Wi' his proud, independant stomach,
    Could ill agree;
So, row't his hurdies in a *hammock*,
      An' owre the Sea.

He ne'er was gien to great misguidin,
Yet coin his pouches wad na bide in;
Wi' him it ne'er was *under hidin*;
    He dealt it free:
The *Muse* was a' that he took pride in,
      That's owre the Sea.

Jamaica bodies, use him weel,
An' hap him in a cozie biel:
Ye'll find him ay a dainty chiel,
    An' fou o' glee:
He wad na wrang'd the vera *Diel*,
      That's owre the Sea.

Fareweel, my *rhyme-composing billie!*
Your native soil was right ill-willie;
But may ye flourish like a lily,
　　　Now bonilie!
I'll toast you in my hindmost *gillie,*
　　　Tho' owre the Sea!

A Dedication to
G**** H******* Esq

Expect na, Sir, in this narration,
A fleechan, fleth'ran *Dedication*,
To roose you up, an' ca' you guid,
An' sprung o' great an' noble bluid;
Because ye're sirnam'd like *His Grace*,
Perhaps related to the race:
Then when I'm tir'd – and sae are *ye*,
Wi' monie a fulsome, sinfu' lie,
Set up a face, how I stop short,
For fear your modesty be hurt.

This may do – maun do, Sir, wi' them wha
Maun please the Great-folk for a wamefou;
For me! sae laigh I need na bow,
For, Lord be thanket, *I can plough*;
And when I downa yoke a naig,
Then, Lord be thanket, *I can beg*;
Sae I shall say, an' that's nae flatt'rin,
It's just *sic Poet* an' *sic Patron*.

The Poet, some guid Angel help him,
Or else, I fear, some *ill ane* skelp him!
He may do weel for a' he's done yet,
But only – he's no just begun yet.

The Patron, (Sir, ye maun forgie me,
I winna lie, come what will o' me)
On ev'ry hand it will allow'd be,
He's just – nae better than he should be.

I readily and freely grant,
He downa see a poor man want;
What's no his ain, he winna tak it;
What ance he says, he winna break it;
Ought he can lend he'll no refus't,
Till aft his guidness is abus'd;
And rascals whyles that do him wrang,
Ev'n *that*, he does na mind it lang:
As Master, Landlord, Husband, Father,
He does na fail his part in either.

But then, nae thanks to him for a' that;
Nae *godly symptom* ye can ca' that;
It's naething but a milder feature,
Of our poor, sinfu', corrupt Nature:
Ye'll get the best o' moral works,
'Mang black *Gentoos*, and Pagan *Turks*,
Or Hunters wild on *Ponotaxi*,
Wha never heard of Orth-d-xy.
That he's the poor man's friend in need,
The Gentleman in word and deed,
It's no through terror of D-mn-t-n;
It's just a carnal inclination,
And Och! that's nae r-g-n-r-t-n!

Morality, thou deadly bane,
Thy tens o' thousands thou hast slain!
Vain is his hope, whase stay an' trust is
In *moral* Mercy, Truth and Justice!

No – stretch a point to catch a plack;
Abuse a Brother to his back;
Steal thro' the *winnock* frae a wh-re,
But point the Rake that taks the *door*;

Be to the Poor like onie whunstane,
And haud their noses to the grunstane;
Ply ev'ry art o' *legal* thieving;
No matter – stick to *sound believing*.

Learn three-mile pray'rs, an' half-mile graces,
Wi' weel spread looves, an' lang, wry faces;
Grunt up a solemn, lengthen'd groan,
And damn a' Parties but your own;
I'll warrant then, ye're nae Deceiver,
A steady, sturdy, staunch *Believer*.

O ye wha leave the springs o' C-lv-n,
For *gumlie dubs* of your ain delvin!
Ye sons of Heresy and Error,
Ye'll *some day* squeel in quaking terror!
When Vengeance draws the sword in wrath,
And in the fire throws the *sheath*;
When Ruin, with his sweeping *besom*,
Just frets till Heav'n commission gies him;
While o'er the *Harp* pale Misery moans,
And strikes the ever-deep'ning tones,
Still louder shrieks, and heavier groans!

Your pardon, Sir, for this digression,
I maist forgat my *Dedication*;
But when Divinity comes cross me,
My readers then are sure to lose me.

So Sir, you see 'twas nae daft vapour,
But I maturely thought it proper,
When a' my works I did review,
To *dedicate* them, Sir, to you;
Because (ye need na tak it ill)
I thought them something like *yoursel*.

Then patronize them wi' your favor,
And your Petitioner shall ever –
I had amaist said, *ever pray*,
But that's a word I need na say:
For prayin I hae little skill o't;
I'm baith dead-sweer, an' wretched ill o't;
But I'se repeat each poor man's *pray'r*,
That kens or hears about you, Sir –

'May ne'er Misfortune's gowling bark,
Howl thro' the dwelling o' the Clerk!
May ne'er his gen'rous, honest heart,
For that same gen'rous spirit smart!
May K******'s far-honor'd name
Lang beet his hymeneal flame,
Till H*******'s, at least a diz'n,
Are frae their nuptial labors risen:
Five bonie Lasses round their table,
And sev'n braw fellows, stout an' able,
To serve their King an' Country weel,
By word, or pen, or pointed steel!
May Health and Peace, with mutual rays,
Shine on the ev'ning o' his days;
Till his wee, curlie *John's* ier-oe,
When ebbing life nae mair shall flow,
The last, sad, mournful rites bestow!'

I will not wind a lang conclusion,
With complimentary effusion:
But whilst your wishes and endeavours,
Are blest with Fortune's smiles and favours,
I am, Dear Sir, with zeal most fervent,
Your much indebted, humble servant.

But if, which Pow'rs above prevent,
That iron-hearted Carl, *Want*,
Attended, in his grim advances,
By *sad mistakes*, and *black mischances*,
While hopes, and joys, and pleasures fly him,
Make you as poor a dog as I am,
Your *humble servant* then no more;
For who would humbly serve the Poor?
But by a poor man's hopes in Heav'n!
While recollection's pow'r is giv'n,
If, in the vale of humble life,
The victim sad of Fortune's strife,
I, through the tender-gushing tear,
Should recognize my *Master dear*,
If friendless, low, we meet together,
Then, Sir, your hand – my Friend and Brother.

To a Louse

On Seeing one on a Lady's Bonnet at Church

Ha! whare ye gaun, ye crowlan ferlie!
Your impudence protects you sairly:
I canna say but ye strunt rarely,
   Owre *gawze* and *lace*;
Tho' faith, I fear ye dine but sparely,
   On sic a place.

 Ye ugly, creepan, blastet wonner,
Detested, shunn'd, by saunt an' sinner,
How daur ye set your fit upon her,
   Sae fine a *Lady!*
Gae somewhere else and seek your dinner,
   On some poor body.

 Swith, in some beggar's haffet squattle;
There ye may creep, and sprawl, and sprattle,
Wi' ither kindred, jumping cattle,
   In shoals and nations;
Whare *horn* nor *bane* ne'er daur unsettle,
   Your thick plantations.

 Now haud you there, ye're out o' sight,
Below the fatt'rels, snug and tight,
Na faith ye yet! ye'll no be right,
   Till ye've got on it,
The vera tapmost, towrin height
   O' *Miss's bonnet.*

My sooth! right bauld ye set your nose out,
As plump an' gray as onie grozet:
O for some rank, mercurial rozet,
   Or fell, red smeddum,
I'd gie you sic a hearty dose o't,
   Wad dress your droddum!

 I wad na been surpriz'd to spy
You on an auld wife's *flainen toy*;
Or aiblins some bit duddie boy,
   On's *wylecoat*;
But Miss's fine *Lunardi*, fye!
   How daur ye do't?

 O *Jenny* dinna toss your head,
An' set your beauties a' abread!
Ye little ken what cursed speed
   The blastie's makin!
Thae *winks* and *finger-ends*, I dread,
   Are notice takin!

 O wad some Pow'r the giftie gie us
To see oursels as others see us!
It wad frae monie a blunder free us
   An' foolish notion:
What airs in dress an' gait wad lea'e us,
   And ev'n Devotion!

*Epistle to J. L*****k*
an old Scotch Bard

April 1st 1785

While briers an' woodbines budding green,
An' Paitricks scraichan loud at e'en,
And morning Poossie whiddan seen,
      Inspire my Muse,
This freedom, in an *unknown* frien',
      I pray excuse.

On Fasteneen we had a rockin,
To ca' the crack and weave our stockin;
And there was muckle fun and jokin,
      Ye need na doubt;
At length we had a hearty yokin,
      At *sang about.*

There was ae *sang*, amang the rest,
Aboon them a' it pleas'd me best,
That some kind husband had addrest,
      To some sweet wife:
It thirl'd the heart-strings thro' the breast,
      A' to the life.

I've scarce heard ought describ'd sae weel,
What gen'rous, manly bosoms feel;
Thought I, 'Can this be *Pope*, or *Steele*,
      Or *Beattie's* wark;'
They told me 'twas an odd kind chiel
      About *Muirkirk.*

It pat me fidgean-fain to hear't,
An' sae about him there I spier't;
Then a' that kent him round declar'd,
    He had *ingine*,
That nane excell'd it, few cam near't,
    It was sae fine.

That set him to a pint of ale,
An' either douse or merry tale,
Or rhymes an' sangs he'd made himsel,
    Or witty catches,
'Tween Inverness and Tiviotdale,
    He had few matches.

Then up I gat, an swoor an aith,
Tho' I should pawn my pleugh an' graith,
Or die a cadger pownie's death,
    At some dyke-back,
A *pint* an' *gill* I'd gie them *baith*,
    To hear your crack.

But first an' foremost, I should tell,
Amaist as soon as I could spell,
I to the *crambo-jingle* fell,
    Tho' rude an' rough,
Yet crooning to a body's sel,
    Does weel eneugh.

I am nae *Poet*, in a sense,
But just a *Rhymer* like by chance,
An' hae to Learning nae pretence,
    Yet, what the matter?
Whene'er my Muse does on me glance,
    I jingle at her.

Your Critic-folk, may cock their nose,
And say, 'How can you e'er propose,
You wha ken hardly *verse* frae *prose*,
   To make a *sang?*'
But by your leaves, my learned foes,
   Ye're maybe wrang.

 What's a' your jargon o' your Schools,
Your Latin names for horns an' stools;
If honest Nature made you *fools*,
   What sairs your Grammars?
Ye'd better taen up *spades* and *shools*,
   Or *knappin-hammers.*

 A set o' dull, conceited Hashes,
Confuse their brains in *Colledge-classes!*
They *gang in* Stirks, and *come out* Asses,
   Plain truth to speak;
An' syne they think to climb Parnassus
   By dint o' Greek!

 Gie me ae spark o' Nature's fire,
That's a' the learning I desire;
Then tho' I drudge thro' dub an' mire
   At pleugh or cart,
My Muse, tho' hamely in attire,
   May touch the heart.

 O for a spunk o' Allan's glee,
Or Ferguson's, the bauld an' slee,
Or bright L*****k's, my friend to be,
   If I can hit it!
That would be *lear* eneugh for me,
   If I could get it.

Now, Sir, if ye hae friends enow,
Tho' *real friends* I b'lieve are few,
Yet, if your catalogue be fow,
   I'se no insist;
But gif ye want ae friend that's true,
   I'm on your list.

I winna blaw about *mysel*,
As ill I like my fauts to tell;
But friends an' folk that wish me well,
   They sometimes roose me;
Tho' I maun own, as monie still,
   As far abuse me.

There's ae *wee faut* they whiles lay to me,
I like the lasses – Gude forgie me!
For monie a Plack they wheedle frae me,
   At dance or fair:
Maybe some *ither thing* they gie me
   They weel can spare.

But Mauchline Race or Mauchline Fair,
I should be proud to meet you there;
We'fe gie ae' night's discharge to *care*,
   If we forgather,
An' hae a swap o' *rhymin-ware*,
   Wi' ane anither.

The *four-gill chap*, we'se gar him clatter,
An' kirs'n him wi' reekin water;
Syne we'll sit down an' tak our whitter,
   To chear our heart;
An' faith, we'se be *acquainted* better
   Before we part.

Awa ye selfish, warly race,
Wha think that havins, sense an' grace,
Ev'n love an' friendship should give place
   To *catch-the-plack!*
I dinna like to see your face,
    Nor hear your crack.

But ye whom social pleasure charms,
Whose hearts the *tide of kindness* warms,
Who hold your *being* on the terms,
   'Each aid the others,'
Come to my bowl, come to my arms,
    My friends, my brothers!

But to conclude my lang epistle,
As my auld pen's worn to the grissle;
Twa lines frae you wad gar me fissle,
   Who am, most fervent,
While I can either sing, or whissle,
    Your friend and servant.

TO THE SAME
April 21st 1785

While new-ca'd kye rowte at the stake,
An' pownies reek in pleugh or braik,
This hour on e'enin's edge I take,
   To own I'm debtor,
To honest-hearted, auld L*****k,
    For his kind *letter*.

Forjesket sair, with weary legs,
Rattlin the corn out-owre the rigs,
Or dealing thro' amang the naigs
   Their ten-hours bite,
My awkart Muse sair pleads and begs,
   I would na write.

 The tapetless, ramseezl'd hizzie,
She's saft at best an' something lazy,
Quo' she, 'Ye ken we've been sae busy
   This month an' mair,
That trouth, my head is grown right dizzie,
   An' something sair.'

 Her dowf excuses pat me mad;
'Conscience,' says I, 'ye thowless jad!
I'll write, an' that a hearty blaud,
   This vera night;
So dinna ye affront your trade,
   But rhyme it right.

 Shall bauld L*****k, the *king o' hearts*,
Tho' mankind were a *pack o' cartes*,
Roose you sae weel for your deserts,
   In terms sae friendly,
Yet ye'll neglect to shaw your parts
   An' thank him kindly?'

 Sae I gat paper in a blink,
An, down gaed *slumpie* in the ink:
Quoth I, 'Before I sleep a wink,
   I vow I'll close it;
An' if ye winna mak it clink,
   By Jove I'll prose it!'

Sae I've begun to scrawl, but whether
In rhyme, or prose, or baith thegither,
Or some hotch-potch that's rightly neither,
      Let time mak proof;
But I shall scribble down some blether
      Just clean ass-loof.

My worthy friend, ne'er grudge an' carp,
Tho' Fortune use you hard an' sharp;
Come, kittle up your *moorlan harp*
      Wi' gleesome touch!
Ne'er mind how Fortune *waft* an' *warp*;
      She's but a b-tch.

She's gien me monie a jirt an' fleg,
Sin I could striddle owre a rig;
But by the L—d, tho' I should beg
      Wi' lyart pow,
I'll laugh, an' sing, an' shake my leg,
      As lang's I dow!

Now comes the *sax an' twentieth* simmer,
I've seen the bud upo' the timmer,
Still persecuted by the limmer
      Frae year to year;
But yet, despite the kittle kimmer,
      I, Rob, am here.

Do ye envy the *city-gent*,
Behint a kist to lie an' sklent,
Or purse-proud, big wi' cent per cent,
      An' muckle wame,
In some bit *Brugh* to represent
      A *Baillie's* name?

Or is't the paughty, feudal *Thane*,
Wi' ruffl'd sark an' glancin cane,
Wha thinks himsel nae *sheep-shank bane*,
            But lordly stalks,
While caps an' bonnets aff are taen,
            As by he walks?

'O *Thou* wha gies us each guid gift!
Gie me o' *wit* an' *sense* a lift,
Then turn me, if *Thou* please, *adrift*,
            Thro' Scotland wide;
Wi' *cits* nor *lairds* I wadna shift,
            In a' their pride!'

Were this the *charter* of our state,
'On pain o' *hell* be rich an' great,'
Damnation then would be our fate,
            Beyond remead;
But, thanks to *Heav'n*, that's no the gate
            We learn our *creed*.

For thus the royal *Mandate* ran,
When first the human race began,
'The social, friendly, honest man,
            Whate'er he be,
'Tis *he* fulfils *great Nature's plan*,
            And none but *he*.'

O *Mandate*, glorious and divine!
The followers o' the ragged Nine,
Poor, thoughtless devils! yet may shine
            In glorious light,
While sordid sons o' Mammon's line
            Are dark as night!

Tho' here they scrape, an' squeeze, an' growl,
Their worthless nievefu' of a *soul*,
May in some *future carcase* howl,
      The forest's fright;
Or in some day-detesting *owl*
      May shun the light.

   Then may L*****k and B**** arise,
To reach their native, kindred skies,
And *sing* their pleasures, hopes an' joys,
      In some mild sphere,
Still closer knit in friendship's ties
      Each passing year!

To W. S*****n, Ochiltree

May – 1785

I Gat your letter, winsome Willie;
Wi' gratefu' heart I thank you brawlie;
Tho' I maun say't, I wad be silly,
        An' unco vain,
Should I believe, my coaxin billie,
        Your flatterin strain.

But I'se believe ye kindly meant it,
I sud be laith to think ye hinted
Ironic satire, sidelins sklented,
        On my poor Musie;
Tho' in sic phraisin terms ye've penn'd it,
        I scarce excuse ye.

My senses wad be in a creel,
Should I but dare a *hope* to speel,
Wi' *Allan*, or wi' *Gilbertfield*,
        The braes o' fame;
Or *Ferguson*, the writer-chiel,
        A deathless name.

(O *Ferguson!* thy glorious *parts*,
Ill-suited *law's* dry, musty arts!
My curse upon your whunstane hearts,
        Ye Enbrugh Gentry!
The tythe o' what ye waste at *cartes*
        Wad stow'd his pantry!)

Yet when a tale comes i' my head,
Or lasses gie my heart a screed,
As whiles they're like to be my dead,

(O sad disease!)
I kittle up my *rustic reed*;
      It gies me ease.

    Auld Coila, now, may fidge fu' fain,
She's gotten *Bardies* o' her ain,
Chiels wha their chanters winna hain,
      But tune their lays,
Till echoes a' resound again
      Her weel-sung praise.

    Nae *Poet* thought her worth his while,
To set her name in measur'd style;
She lay like some unkend-of isle
      Beside *New Holland*,
Or whare wild-meeting oceans *boil*
      Besouth *Magellan*.

    Ramsay an' famous *Ferguson*
Gied *Forth* an' *Tay* a lift aboon;
Yarrow an' *Tweed*, to monie a tune,
      Owre Scotland rings,
While *Irwin, Lugar, Aire* an' *Doon*,
      Naebody sings.

    Th' *Illissus, Tiber, Thames* an' *Seine*,
Glide sweet in monie a tunefu' line;
But *Willie* set your fit to mine,
      An' cock your crest,
We'll gar our streams an' burnies shine
      Up wi' the best.

    We'll sing auld Coila's plains an' fells,
Her moors red-brown wi' heather bells,
Her banks an' braes, her dens an' dells,

Where glorious Wallace
Aft bure the gree, as story tells,
    Frae Suthron billies.

  At Wallace' name, what Scottish blood,
But boils up in a spring-tide flood!
Oft have our fearless fathers strode
    By Wallace' side,
Still pressing onward, red-wat-shod,
    Or glorious dy'd!

  O sweet are Coila's haughs an' woods,
When lintwhites chant amang the buds,
And jinkin hares, in amorous whids,
    Their loves enjoy,
While thro' the braes the cushat croods
    With wailfu' cry!

  Ev'n winter bleak has charms to me,
When winds rave thro' the naked tree;
Or frosts on hills of *Ochiltree*
    Are hoary gray;
Or blinding drifts wild-furious flee,
    Dark'ning the day!

  O Nature! a' thy shews an' forms
To feeling, pensive hearts hae charms!
Whether the Summer kindly warms,
    Wi' life an' light,
Or Winter howls, in gusty storms,
    The lang, dark night!

  The *Muse*, nae *Poet* ever fand her,
Till by himsel he learn'd to wander,
Adown some trottin burn's meander,

An' no think lang;
O sweet, to stray an' pensive ponder
    A heart-felt sang!

   The warly race may drudge an' drive,
Hog-shouther, jundie, stretch an' strive,
Let me fair Nature's face descrive,
    And I, wi' pleasure,
Shall let the busy, grumbling hive
    Bum owre their treasure.

   Fareweel, 'my rhyme-composing' brither!
We've been owre lang unkenn'd to ither:
Now let us lay our heads thegither,
    In love fraternal:
May *Envy* wallop in a tether,
    Black fiend, infernal!

   While Highlandmen hate tolls an' taxes;
While moorlan herds like guid, fat braxies;
While Terra firma, on her axis,
    Diurnal turns,
Count on a friend, in faith an' practice,
    In Robert Burns.

POSTSCRIPT

My memory's no worth a preen;
I had amaist forgotten clean,
Ye bad me write you what they mean
    By this *new-light,*
'Bout which our *herds* sae aft hae been
    Maist like to fight.

---

* A cant-term for those religious opinions, which Dr Taylor of Norwich has defended so strenuously.

In days when mankind were but callans,
At *Grammar, Logic,* an' sic talents,
They took nae pains their speech to balance,
      Or rules to gie,
But spak their thoughts in plain, braid lallans,
      Like you or me.

In thae auld times, they thought the *Moon,*
Just like a sark, or pair o' shoon,
Woor by degrees, till her last roon
      Gaed past their viewin,
An' shortly after she was done
      They gat a new ane.

This past for certain, undisputed;
It ne'er cam i' their heads to doubt it,
Till chiels gat up an' wad confute it,
      An' ca'd it wrang;
An' muckle din there was about it,
      Baith loud an' lang.

Some *herds*, weel learn'd upo' the beuk,
Wad threap auld folk the thing misteuk;
For 'twas the *auld moon* turn'd a newk
      An' out o' sight,
An' backlins-comin, to the leuk,
      She grew mair bright.

This was deny'd, it was affirm'd;
The *herds* an' *hissels* were alarm'd;
The rev'rend gray-beards rav'd an' storm'd,
      That beardless laddies
Should think they better were inform'd,
      Than their auld dadies.

Frae less to mair it gaed to sticks;
Frae words an' aiths to clours an' nicks;
An' monie a fallow gat his licks,
      Wi' hearty crunt;
An' some, to learn them for their tricks,
      Were hang'd an' brunt.

This game was play'd in monie lands,
An' *auld-light* caddies bure sic hands,
That faith, the *youngsters* took the sands
      Wi' nimble shanks,
Till *Lairds* forbad, by strict commands,
      Sic bluidy pranks.

But *new-light herds* gat sic a cowe,
Folk thought them ruin'd stick-an-stowe,
Till now amaist on ev'ry *knowe*
      Ye'll find ane plac'd;
An' some, their *New-light* fair avow,
      Just quite barefac'd.

Nae doubt the *auld-light flocks* are bleatan;
Their zealous *herds* are vex'd an' sweatan;
Mysel, I've ev'n seen them greetan
      Wi' girnan spite,
To hear the *Moon* sae sadly lie'd on
      By word an' write.

But shortly they will cowe the louns!
Some *auld-light herds* in neebor towns
Are mind't, in things they ca' *balloons*,
      To tak a flight,
An' stay ae month amang the *Moons*
      An' see them right.

Guid observation they will gie them;
An' when the *auld Moon's* gaun to le'ae them,
The hindmost *shaird*, they'll fetch it wi' them,
Just i' their pouch,
An' when the *new-light* billies see them,
I think they'll crouch!

Sae, ye observe that a' this clatter
Is naething but a 'moonshine matter';
But tho' dull *prose-folk* latin splatter
In logic tulzie,
I hope we, *Bardies*, ken some better
Than mind sic brulzie.

*Epistle to J. R*******
enclosing some Poems

O Rough, rude, ready-witted R******,
The wale o' cocks for fun an' drinkin!
There's monie godly folks are thinkin,
        Your *dreams** an' tricks
Will send you, Korah-like, a sinkin,
        Straught to auld Nick's.

Ye hae sae monie cracks an' cants,
And in your wicked, druken rants,
Ye mak a devil o' the *Saunts*,
        An' fill them fou;
And then their failings, flaws an' wants,
        Are a' seen thro'.

Hypocrisy, in mercy spare it!
That *holy robe*, O dinna tear it!
Spare't for their sakes wha aften wear it,
        The lads in *black*;
But your curst wit, when it comes near it,
        Rives't aff their back.

Think, wicked Sinner, wha ye're skaithing:
It's just the *Blue-gown* badge an' claithing,
O' Saunts; take that, ye lea'e them naething,
        To ken them by,
Frae ony unregenerate Heathen,
        Like you or I.

---

* A certain humorous *dream* of his was then making a noise in the world.

I've sent you here, some rhymin ware,
A' that I bargain'd for, an' mair;
Sae when ye hae an hour to spare,
    I will expect,
Yon *Sang** ye'll sen't, wi' cannie care,
    And no neglect.

Tho' faith, sma' heart hae I to sing!
My Muse dow scarcely spread her wing:
I've play'd mysel a bonie *spring*,
    An *danc'd* my fill!
I'd better gaen an' sair't the king,
    At Bunker's hill.

'Twas ae night lately, in my fun,
I gaed a rovin wi' the gun,
An' brought a *Paitrick* to the *grun'*,
    A bonie *hen*,
And, as the twilight was begun,
    Thought nane wad ken.

The poor, wee thing was *little hurt*;
I *straiket* it a wee for sport,
Ne'er thinkan they wad fash me for't;
    But, Deil-ma-care!
Somebody tells the *Poacher-Court*,
    The hale affair.

Some auld, us'd hands had taen a note,
That *sic a hen* had got a *shot*;
I was suspected for the plot;

---

* A *Song* he had promised the Author.

I scorn'd to lie;
So gat the whissle o' my groat,
An' pay't the *fee*.

But by my *gun*, o' guns the wale,
An' by my *pouther* an' my *hail*,
An' by my *hen*, an' by her *tail*,
I vow an' swear!
The *Game* shall Pay, owre moor an' *dail*,
For this, niest year.

As soon's the *clockin-time* is by,
An' the *wee powts* begun to cry,
L—d, I'se hae sportin by an' by,
For my *gowd guinea*;
Tho' I should herd the *buckskin* kye
For't, in Virginia!

Trowth, they had muckle for to blame!
'Twas neither broken wing nor limb,
But twa-three *draps* about the *wame*
Scarce thro' the *feathers*;
An' baith a *yellow George* to claim,
An' *thole* their *blethers!*

It pits me ay as mad's a hare;
So I can rhyme nor write nae mair;
But *pennyworths* again is fair,
When time's expedient:
Meanwhile I am, respected Sir,
Your most obedient.

Song

Tune: Corn rigs are bonie

I

It was upon a Lammas night,
    When corn rigs are bonie,
Beneath the moon's unclouded light,
    I held awa to Annie:
The time flew by, wi' tentless head,
    Till 'tween the late and early;
Wi' sma' persuasion she agreed,
    To see me thro' the barley.

II

The sky was blue, the wind was still,
    The moon was shining clearly;
I set her down, wi' right good will,
    Amang the rigs o' barley:
I ken't her heart was a' my ain;
    I lov'd her most sincerely;
I kiss'd her owre and owre again,
    Amang the rigs o' barley.

III

I lock'd her in my fond embrace;
    Her heart was beating rarely:
My blessings on that happy place,
    Amang the rigs o' barley!
But by the moon and stars so bright,
    That shone that night so clearly!
She ay shall bless that happy night,
    Amang the rigs o' barley.

IV

I hae been blythe wi' Comrades dear;
   I hae been merry drinking;
I hae been joyfu' gath'rin gear;
   I hae been happy thinking:
But a' the pleasures e'er I saw,
   Tho' three times doubl'd fairly,
That happy night was worth them a',
   Amang the rigs o' barley.

CHORUS

Corn rigs, an' barley rigs,
   An' corn rigs are bonie:
I'll ne'er forget that happy night,
   Amang the rigs wi' Annie.

Song
composed in August

Tune: I had a horse, I had nae mair

I

Now westlin winds, and slaught'ring guns
 Bring Autumn's pleasant weather;
And the moorcock springs, on whirring wings,
 Amang the blooming heather:
Now waving grain, wide o'er the plain,
 Delights the weary Farmer;
And the moon shines bright, when I rove at night,
 To muse upon my Charmer.

II

The Partridge loves the fruitful fells;
 The Plover loves the mountains;
The Woodcock haunts the lonely dells;
 The soaring Hern the fountains:
Thro' lofty groves, the Cushat roves,
 The path of man to shun it;
The hazel bush o'erhangs the Thrush,
 The spreading thorn the Linnet.

III

Thus ev'ry kind their pleasure find,
 The savage and the tender;
Some social join, and leagues combine;
 Some solitary wander:
Avaunt, away! the cruel sway,
 Tyrannic man's dominion;
The Sportsman's joy, the murd'ring cry,
 The flutt'ring, gory pinion!

IV

But Peggy dear, the ev'ning's clear,
　　Thick flies the skimming Swallow;
The sky is blue, the fields in view,
　　All fading-green and yellow:
Come let us stray our gladsome way,
　　And view the charms of Nature;
The rustling corn, the fruited thorn,
　　And ev'ry happy creature.

V

We'll gently walk, and sweetly talk,
　　Till the silent moon shine clearly;
I'll grasp thy waist, and fondly prest,
　　Swear how I love thee dearly:
Not vernal show'rs to budding flow'rs,
　　Not Autumn to the Farmer,
So dear can be, as thou to me,
　　My fair, my lovely Charmer!

Song

Tune: Gilderoy

I

From thee, Eliza, I must go,
 And from my native shore:
The cruel fates between us throw
 A boundless ocean's roar;
But boundless oceans, roaring wide,
 Between my Love and me,
They never, never can divide
 My heart and soul from thee.

II

Farewell, farewell, Eliza dear,
 The maid that I adore!
A boding voice is in mine ear,
 We part to meet no more!
But the latest throb that leaves my heart,
 While Death stands victor by,
That throb, Eliza, is thy part,
 And thine that latest sigh!

The Farewell
to the Brethren of St James's Lodge, Tarbolton

Tune: Goodnight and joy be wi' you a'

I

Adieu! a heart-warm, fond adieu!
   Dear brothers of the *mystic tye!*
Ye favored, *enlighten'd* Few,
   Companions of my social joy!
Tho' I to foreign lands must hie,
   Pursuing Fortune's slidd'ry ba',
With melting heart, and brimful eye,
   I'll mind you still, tho' far awa.

II

Oft have I met your social Band,
   And spent the chearful, festive night;
Oft, honor'd with supreme command,
   Presided o'er the *Sons of light*:
And by that *Hieroglyphic* bright,
   Which none but *Craftsmen* ever saw!
Strong Mem'ry on my heart shall write
   Those happy scenes when far awa!

III

May Freedom, Harmony and Love
   Unite you in the *grand Design,*
Beneath th' Omniscient Eye above,
   The glorious Architect Divine!

That you may keep th' *unerring line*,
  Still rising by the *plummet's law*,
Till *Order* bright, completely shine,
  Shall be my Pray'r when far awa.

IV

And *you*, farewell! whose merits claim,
  Justly that *highest badge* to wear!
Heav'n bless your honor'd, noble Name,
  To Masonry and Scotia dear!
A last request, permit me here,
  When yearly ye assemble a',
One *round*, I ask it with a *tear*,
  To him, *the Bard, that's far awa.*

EPITAPH ON A HENPECKED COUNTRY SQUIRE

As father Adam first was fool'd,
  A case that's still too common,
Here lyes a man a woman rul'd,
  The devil rul'd the woman.

EPIGRAM ON SAID OCCASION

O Death, hadst thou but spar'd his life,
  Whom we, this day, lament!
We freely wad exchang'd the *wife*,
  An' a' been weel content.

Ev'n as he is, cauld in his graff,
  The *swap* we yet will do't;
Tak thou the Carlin's carcase aff,
  Thou'se get the *saul* o' *boot.*

ANOTHER

One Queen Artemisa, as old stories tell,
When depriv'd of her husband she loved so well,
In respect for the love and affection he'd show'd her,
She reduc'd him to dust, and she drank up the Powder.
But Queen N********** of a diff'rent complexion,
When call'd on to order the fun'ral direction,
Would have *eat* her dead lord, on a slender pretence,
Not to show her respect, but – *to save the expence.*

Epitaphs

ON A CELEBRATED RULING ELDER

Here Sowter **** in Death does sleep;
    To H—ll, if he's gane thither,
Satan, gie him thy gear to keep,
    He'll haud it weel thegither.

ON A NOISY POLEMIC

Below thir stanes lie Jamie's banes;
    O Death, it's my opinion,
Thou ne'er took such a bleth'ran b—tch,
    Into thy dark dominion!

ON WEE JOHNIE
Hic jacet wee *Johnie*

Whoe'er thou art, O reader, know,
    That Death has murder'd Johnie;
An' here his *body* lies fu' low –
    For *saul* he ne'er had ony.

FOR THE AUTHOR'S FATHER

O ye whose cheek the tear of pity stains,
    Draw near with pious rev'rence and attend!
Here lie the loving Husband's dear remains,
    The tender Father, and the gen'rous Friend.

The pitying Heart that felt for human Woe;
  The dauntless heart that fear'd no human Pride;
The Friend of Man, to vice alone a foe;
  'For ev'n his failings lean'd to Virtue's side.'*

FOR R. A. ESQ
  Know thou, O stranger to the fame
Of this much lov'd, much honor'd name!
(For none that knew him need be told)
A warmer heart Death ne'er made cold.

FOR G. H. ESQ
The poor man weeps – here G—N sleeps,
  Whom canting wretches blam'd:
But with *such as he*, where'er he be.
  May I be *sav'd* or *d—'d!*

* Goldsmith.

A Bard's Epitaph

Is there a whim-inspir'd fool,
Owre fast for thought, owre hot for rule,
Owre blate to seek, owre proud to snool,
    Let him draw near;
And o'er this grassy heap sing dool,
    And drap a tear.

Is there a Bard of rustic song,
Who, noteless, steals the crouds among
That weekly this area throng,
    O, pass not by!
But with a frater-feeling strong,
    Here, heave a sigh.

Is there a man whose judgment clear,
Can others teach the course to steer,
Yet runs, himself, life's mad career,
    Wild as the wave,
Here pause – and thro' the starting tear,
    Survey this grave.

The poor Inhabitant below
Was quick to learn and wise to know,
And keenly felt the friendly glow,
    And *softer flame*;
But thoughtless follies laid him low,
    And stain'd his name!

Reader attend – whether thy soul
Soars fancy's flights beyond the pole,
Or darkling grubs this earthly hole,

In low pursuit,
Know, prudent, cautious, *self-controul*
Is Wisdom's root.

FINIS

GLOSSARY

Words that are universally known, and those that differ from the English only by the elision of letters by apostrophes, or by varying the termination of the verb, are not inserted. The terminations may be thus known; the participle present, instead of *ing*, ends, in the Scotch Dialect, in *an* or *in*; in *an*, particularly, when the verb is composed of the participle present, and any of the tenses of the auxiliary, *to be*. The past time and participle past are usually made by shortening the *ed* into *'t*.

Aback, behind, away
Abiegh, at a distance
Ae, one
Agley, wide of the aim
Aiver, an old horse
Aizle, a red ember
Ane, one, an
Ase, ashes
Ava, at all, of all
Awn, the beard of oats, &c.

Bairan, baring
Banie, bony
Baws'nt, having a white stripe down the face
Ben, *but and ben*, the country kitchen and parlour
Bellys, bellows
Bee, *to let bee*, to leave in quiet
Biggin, a building
Bield, shelter
Blastet, worthless
Blather, the bladder

Blink, a glance, an amorous leer, a short space of time
Blype, a shred of cloth, &c.
Boost, behoved
Brash, a sudden illness
Brat, a worn shred of Cloth
Brainge, to draw unsteadily
Braxie, a morkin sheep
Brogue, an affront
Breef, an invulnerable charm
Breastet, sprung forward
Burnewin, *q. d.* burn the wind, a Blacksmith.

Ca', to call, to drive
Caup, a small, wooden dish with two lugs, or handles
Cape stane, cope stone
Cairds, tinkers
Cairn, a loose heap of stones
Chuffie, fat-faced
Collie, a general and sometimes a particular name for country curs

Cog, or coggie, a small wooden dish without handles

Cootie, a pretty large wooden dish

Crack, conversation, to converse

Crank, a harsh, grating sound

Crankous, fretting, peevish

Croon, a hollow, continued moan

Crowl, to creep

Crouchie, crook-backed

Cranreuch, the hoar frost

Curpan, the crupper

Cummock, a short staff

Daud, the noise of one falling flat, a large piece of bread, &c.

Daut, to caress, to fondle

Daimen, now and then, seldom

Daurk, a day's labour

Deleeret, delirious

Dead-sweer, very loath, averse

Dowie, crazy and dull

Donsie, unlucky, dangerous

Doylte, stupified, hebetated

Dow, am able

Dought, was able

Doyte, to go drunkenly or stupidly

Drummock, meal and water mixed raw

Drunt, pet, pettish humor

Dush, to push as a bull, ram, &c.

Duds, rags of clothes

Eerie, frighted; particularly the dread of spirits

Eldritch, fearful, horrid, ghastly

Eild, old age

Eydent, constant, busy

Fa', fall, lot

Fawsont, decent, orderly

Faem, foam

Fatt'rels, ribband ends, &c.

Ferlie, a wonder, to wonder; also a term of contempt

Fecht, to fight

Fetch, to stop suddenly in the draught, and then come on too hastily

Fier, sound, healthy

Fittie lan', the near horse of the hindmost pair in the plough

Flunkies, livery servants

Fley, to frighten

Fleesh, fleece

Flisk, to fret at the yoke

Flichter, to flutter

Forbears, ancestors

Forby, besides

Forjesket, jaded

Fow, full, drunk; a bushel, &c.

Freath, froath

Fuff, to blow intermittedly

Fyle, to dirty, to soil

Gash, wise, sagacious, talkative; to converse

Gate, or gact, way, manner, practice

Gab, the mouth; to speak boldly

Gawsie, jolly, large

Geck, to toss the head in pride or wantonness

Gizz, a wig

Gilpey, a young girl

Glaizie, smooth, glittering

Glunch, a frown; to frown

Glint, to peep

Grushie, of thick, stout growth

Gruntle, the visage; a grunting noise

Grousome, loathsomely grim

Hal, or hald, hold, biding place

Hash, a term of contempt

Haverel, a quarter-wit

Haurl, to drag, to peel

Hain, to save, to spare

Heugh, a crag, a coal pit

Hecht, to forebode

Histie, dry, chapt, barren

Howe, hollow

Hoste or Hoast, to cough

Howk, to dig

Hoddan, the motion of a sage country farmer on an old cart horse

Houghmagandie, a species of gender composed of the masculine and feminine united

Hoy, to urge incessantly

Hoyte, a motion between a trot and a gallop

Hogshouther, to justle with the shoulder

Icker, an ear of corn

Ier-oe, a great grand child

Ingine, genius

Ill-willie, malicious, unkind

Jauk, to dally at work

Jouk, to stoop

Jocteleg, a kind of knife

Jundie, to justle

Kae, a daw

Ket, a hairy, ragged fleece of wool

Kiutle, to cuddle, to caress, to fondle

Kiaugh, carking anxiety

Kirsen, to christen

Laggen, the angle at the bottom of a wooden dish

Laithfu', bashful

Leeze me, a term of congratulatory endearment

Leal, loyal, true

Loot, did let

Lowe, flame; to flame

Lunt, smoke; to smoke

Limmer, a woman of easy virtue

Link, to trip along

Lyart, grey

Luggie, a small, wooden dish with one handle

Manteele, a mantle

Melvie, to soil with meal

Mense, good breeding

Mell, to meddle with

Modewurk, a mole

Moop, to nibble as a sheep

Muslin kail, broth made up simply of water, barley and greens

Nowte, black cattle

Nieve, the fist

Owre, over

Outler, lying in the fields, not housed at night

Pack, intimate, familiar

Pang, to cram

Painch, the paunch

Paughty, proud, saucy

Pattle or pettle, the ploughstaff

Peghan, the crop of fowls, the stomach

Penny-wheep, small beer

Pine, pain, care

Pirratch, or porritch, pottage

Pliskie, trick

Primsie, affectedly nice

Prief, proof

Quat, quit, did quit

Quaikin, quaking

Ramfeezl'd, overspent

Raep or rape, a rope

Raucle, stout, clever

Raible, to repeat by rote

Ram-stam, thoughtless

Raught, did reach

Reestet, shrivelled

Reest, to be restive

Reck, to take heed

Rede, counsel, to counsel

Ripp, a handful of unthreshed corn, &c.

Rief, reaving

Risk, to make a noise like the breaking of small roots with the plough

Rowt, to bellow

Roupet, hoarse

Runkle, a wrinkle

Rockin, a meeting on a winter evening

Sair, sore

Saunt, a saint

Scrimp, scant; to stint

Scriegh, to cry shrilly

Scrieve, to run smoothly and swiftly

Screed, to tear

Scawl, a Scold

Sconner, to loath

Sheen, bright

Shaw, a little wood; to show

Shaver, a humorous mischievous wag

Skirl, a shrill cry

Sklent, to slant, to fib

Skiegh, mettlesome, fiery, proud

Slype, to fall over like a wet furrow

Smeddum, powder of any kind

Smytrie, a numerous collection of small individuals

Snick-drawing, trick-contriving

Snash, abusive language

Sowther, to cement, to solder

Splore, a ramble

Spunkie, fiery; will o' wisp

Spairge, to spurt about like water or mire, to soil

Sprittie, rushy

Squatter, to flutter in water

Staggie, diminutive of Stag

Steeve, firm

Stank, a pool of standing water

Stroan, to pour out like a spout

Stegh, to cram the belly

Stibble-rig, the reaper who takes the lead

Sten, to rear as a horse

Swith, get away

Syne, since, ago, then

Tapetless, unthinking

Tawie, that handles quietly

Tawted, or tawtet, matted together

Taet, a small quantity

Tarrow, to murmur at one's allowance

Thowless, slack, pithless

Thack an' raep, all kinds of necessaries, particularly clothes

Thowe, thaw

Tirl, to knock gently, to uncover

Toyte, to walk like old age

Trashtrie, trash

Wauket, thickened as fullers do cloth

Water-kelpies, a sort of mischievous spirits that are said to haunt fords, &c.

Water-brose, brose made simply of meal and water

Wauble, to swing

Wair, to lay out, to spend

Whaizle, to wheez

Whisk, to sweep

Wintle, a wavering, swinging motion

Wiel, a small whirlpool

Winze, an oath

Wonner, wonder, a term of contempt

Wooer-bab, the garter knotted below the knee with a couple of loops and ends

Wrack, to vex, to trouble

Yell, dry, spoken of a cow

Ye, is frequently used for the singular

Young-guidman, a new married man

A NOTE ON THE TEXT

Robert Burns (1759–96) made a decisive mark with *Poems, Chiefly in the Scottish Dialect* (1786). As Hugh MacDiarmid has written, 'it was the volume by which, quite deliberately, Burns aimed at, and secured, recognition not as a local bard but as a great poet.' It was printed by John Wilson of Kilmarnock in 1786. Scottish publishing evolved differently from English. In eighteenth-century London, booksellers and stationers (eventually publishers) gained ascendancy over printers. Authors had a limited remit and no protection until the Copyright Act of 1720. In Scotland respectable printers affixed their name, not a bookseller's or publisher's, to a title page: Robert Urie in Glasgow, or Robert and Andrew Foulis with their classic list, or John Wilson of Kilmarnock.

Burns first circulated to potential subscribers and patrons a proposal for a volume of 'Scotch' poems; then – considering a wider readership – he decided to add English work. He composed a Preface addressed not to specialist or local readers but to a more general public. He played up to the image of himself as 'the simple Bard, unbroke by rules of Art': in fact he was an excellent technician who also wrote a vivid, very clear and well-instructed prose style. He must have been a little wary of the rustic packaging he had himself chosen, writing from Mossgiel in April 1786 to John Arnott, enclosing a subscription bill for the first edition: 'I should be much hurt, Sir, if anyone should view my poor Parnassian Pegasus in the light of a spur-galled Hack, and think that I wish to make a shilling or two by him.' The letter continues with a touching and funny account of the loss of his 'wife' Jean Armour, whose pregnancy, delivery of twins and the scandal of their adultery coincided with publication and rather stole from the pleasure of his first appearance between boards. Also from Mossgiel on 12 June 1786, to his friend the shoemaker David Brice in Glasgow, he confided the consequences of his adultery, then adds: 'You will have heard that I am going to commence poet in print; and to-morrow my works go to the press. I expect it will be a volume of about two hundred pages' (in the end it was 240) '– it is just the last foolish action I intend to do; and then turn a wiser man as fast as possible.' Then to John Richmond on 9 July he wrote: 'My book will be ready in a fortnight. If you have any subscribers return them by Connell (the carrier).'

Wilson printed 612 copies of *Poems* on 31 July: 350 went to subscribers, committed to purchase in advance; the rest were sold at those subscribers' recommendation. Three weeks after publication, only thirteen copies remained. No review copies as such were sent out. Marketing was unnecessary: the poet's following, especially in Ayrshire, supported him.

He was in effect his own editor for *Poems*, the printer taking little interest in the actual texts of what he was producing. This was as it should be in the case of so original a writer: his friends and critics were keen to make him more 'correct' in every respect, from his language to his morality, and later changes are not invariably for the better.

How close were his relations with the printer Wilson? Certain tensions are to be detected. In October, after the book was published, he wrote to Robert Aiken: 'I was with Wilson, my printer, t'other day, and settled all our bygone matters between us. After I had paid him all demands, I made him the offer of the second edition, on the hazard of being paid out of the first and readiest, which he declines.' Wilson's costings for a second printing say much about the disparity between materials and labour costs at the time.

By his account, the paper of a thousand copies would cost about twenty-seven pounds, and the printing about fifteen or sixteen: he offers to agree to this for the printing, if I will advance for the paper, but this you know is out of my power; so farewell hopes of a second edition till I grow richer! an epocha which, I think, will arrive at the payment of the British national debt.

Given the success of the first edition, he was deeply troubled not to be able to go to a second.

The next year he sold the copyright in *Poems* to William Creech, of Edinburgh, for 100 guineas. It was a serious mistake, and like all such mistakes dictated by necessity rather than prudence.

Michael Schmidt